INVESTMENT INCENTIVES
AND DISINCENTIVES:
EFFECTS
ON INTERNATIONAL DIRECT INVESTMENT

ORGANISATION FOR ECONOMIC CO-OPERATION AND DEVELOPMENT

Pursuant to article 1 of the Convention signed in Paris on 14th December 1960, and which came into force on 30th September 1961, the Organisation for Economic Co-operation and Development (OECD) shall promote policies designed:

- to achieve the highest sustainable economic growth and employment and a rising standard of living in Member countries, while maintaining financial stability, and thus to contribute to the development of the world economy;
- to contribute to sound economic expansion in Member as well as non-member countries in the process of economic development; and
- to contribute to the expansion of world trade on a multilateral, non-discriminatory basis in accordance with international obligations.

The original Member countries of the OECD are Austria, Belgium, Canada, Denmark, France, the Federal Republic of Germany, Greece, Iceland, Ireland, Italy, Luxembourg, the Netherlands, Norway, Portugal, Spain, Sweden, Switzerland, Turkey, the United Kingdom and the United States. The following countries acceded subsequently through accession at the dates indicated hereafter: Japan (28th April 1964), Finland (28th January 1969), Australia (7th June 1971) and New Zealand (29th May 1973).

The Socialist-Federal Republic of Yugoslavia takes part in some of the work of the OECD (agreement of 28th October 1961).

Publié en français sous le titre:

STIMULANTS ET OBSTACLES
A L'INVESTISSEMENT :
EFFETS SUR
L'INVESTISSEMENT DIRECT INTERNATIONAL

In stimulating investment, Member countries rely mainly on macroeconomic policies to set the scene for productive investment in general. They do, nevertheless, offer a considerable array of investment incentives measures the purpose of which is to provide additional stimulation or guidance for investments in particular areas or directions. Member countries also operate other measures, generally geared to ensuring particular benefits to host countries but which may however have disincentive effects on international direct investment.

This report, which updates and augments the 1983 OECD publication, examines in Chapter I the main patterns regarding the provision of incentives and disincentives, including changing orientations in their use and administration. The report assesses in Chapter II, the effects of incentives and disincentives on international direct investment patterns, building upon the 1983 analysis and focusing on effects of recent important developments, including trade–related investment measures, which are now being discussed in the Uruguay Round negotiations.

In its analysis of patterns and trends, the report shows that there is continued broad use of investment incentives but that there is less overall expenditure associated with their use. A reorientation, or realignment of investment incentives has also taken place with continuing emphasis, for example, on positive rather than defensive measures, and measures which work with market forces in order that investment decisions are made more on the basis of commercial considerations, with less distortion to investment patterns. There is also an evident trend away from horizontal, sector–wide schemes to vertical ones, for example, promoting the use of new technologies. The administration of investment incentives has generally been simplified and there is also a greater emphasis on investments displaying need for assistance and where the economy is likely to benefit from the outlay.

In the case of disincentives, at least for OECD countries, there has been considerable progress in the relaxation or abandonment of disincentives indicating a greater emphasis on attracting international direct investment through the removal of restrictions.

Although investment incentives may have various effects on international direct investment patterns, they are not generally felt to be one of the key determinants of overall investment levels. They can, however, have a stronger influence on decisions related to location, size and timing of investments. Disincentives may have wider, more diverse effects than incentives and impact on more components of the overall investment decision including, for example, its form and purchasing and sales patterns. Disincentives, including trade–related investment measures, are an important element of investor's perception of the investment climate and particularly when associated with incentives, can result in important distortions of investment and trade–related patterns. They often are an important element of investors' perception of the investment climate.

This report has been conducted by the OECD's Committee on International Investment and Multinational Enterprises which approved the report in December 1987. It was made available to the public by Decision of the OECD Council on 17th November 1988.

Also available

"INTERNATIONAL INVESTMENT AND MULTINATIONAL ENTERPRISES" series

MINIMIZING CONFLICTING REQUIREMENTS, APPROACHES OF "MODERATION AND RESTRAINT" (October 1987)
(21 87 11 1) ISBN 92-64-13031-4   48 pages   £5.00   US$11.00   FF50.00   DM22.00

STRUCTURE AND ORGANISATION OF MULTINATIONAL ENTERPRISES (November 1987)
(21 87 12 1) ISBN 92-64-13030-6   60 pages   £6.00   US$13.00   FF60.00   DM26.00

RECENT TRENDS IN INTERNATIONAL DIRECT INVESTMENT (June 1987)
(21 87 06 1) ISBN 92-64-12971-5   214 pages   £10.00   US$21.00   FF100.00   DM43.00

THE OECD GUIDELINES FOR MULTINATIONAL ENTERPRISES (April 1986)
(21 86 03 1) ISBN 92-64-12812-3   92 pages   £6.00   US$12.00   FF60.00   DM27.00

NATIONAL TREATMENT FOR FOREIGN-CONTROLLED ENTERPRISES (April 1985)
(21 85 01 1) ISBN 92-64-12658-9   148 pages   £8.00   US$16.00   FF80.00   DM36.00

INVESTMENT INCENTIVES AND DISINCENTIVES AND THE INTERNATIONAL INVESTMENT PROCESS (March 1983)
(21 83 01 1) ISBN 92-64-12400-4   250 pages   £8.60   US$17.00   FF86.00   DM43.00

THE 1984 REVIEW OF THE 1976 DECLARATION AND DECISIONS (July 1984)
(21 84 02 1) ISBN 92-64-12585-X   66 pages   £3.20   US$6.50   FF32.00   DM16.00

* * *

CONTROLS AND IMPEDIMENTS AFFECTING INWARD DIRECT INVESTMENT IN OECD MEMBER COUNTRIES (September 1987)
(21 87 09 1) ISBN 92-64-13005-5   72 pages   £5.00   US$11.00   FF50.00   DM22.00

INTRODUCTION TO THE OECD CODES OF LIBERALISATION-JUNE 1987 (July 1987)
(21 87 07 1) ISBN 92-64-12978-2   42 pages   £3.50   US$7.00   FF35.00   DM75.00

Prices charged at the OECD Bookshop.

*THE OECD CATALOGUE OF PUBLICATIONS and supplements will be sent free of charge
on request addressed either to OECD Publications Service,
2, rue André-Pascal, 75775 PARIS CEDEX 16, or to the OECD Distributor in your country.*

TABLE OF CONTENTS

Chapter I

INVESTMENT INCENTIVES AND DISINCENTIVES

All OECD Member countries employ, to varying degrees, investment incentives measures to promote their objectives in a variety of policy areas such as industry and technology, regional policy, service sector activities and small–firm development. Although more restricted in incidence, a number of OECD countries also apply particular measures which may have a disincentive impact on investment, particularly foreign direct investment. This report discusses the main features of investment incentive and disincentive measures in Member countries (see Section 2) and examines a number of trends with respect to these measures that have been witnessed since the early 1980s (see Section 3). Focusing particularly on the latter, this section summarises the main directions of change.

In stimulating investment, Member countries rely mainly on macroeconomic policies to set the scene for productive investment in general, with investment incentives being used to provide additional stimulation or guidance for investments in particular areas or directions. Before addressing particular features of incentives schemes in specific policy areas, there are a number of broad tendencies which have emerged with respect to the use of investment incentives in general.

There has been a general trend towards some reduction in the overall level of government intervention. On the one hand, this is associated with greater efforts by countries to use general economic policies to improve the economic climate, to encourage growth and to reduce uncertainty and instability. There is a greater reliance on the role of the market to guide investment decisions. On the other hand, for investment incentives, there is increasing emphasis in the criteria determining awards and award levels both to demonstrate need on the part of the project for assistance and to ensure value for money spent through incentives. The latter is sometimes reflected by attempts to use incentives more at the margin as well as by the examination of the viability of the project to be assisted or the requirement to fulfill certain conditions in order to ensure particular benefits. Finally, these programmes have been subject to budgetary restraint pressures that have affected government expenditure in all Member countries.

The administration of investment incentives is also becoming more straightforward, with simpler and more transparent implementation. Not only does this save on the administrative costs of incentives measures but, more particularly, the emphasis has been on improving policy delivery and the productive use of incentives expenditures.

Another main development has been the continuing move from "defensive" to "positive" support policies — i.e., with less intervention in sectors or firms unlikely to become competitive in world markets or to be viable in the longer term (e.g., declining industries). Investment incentives are now more geared to promoting positive structural adjustment and the movement of productive resources to expanding and particularly new generation industries.

In the area of industrial and innovation policies there has been a clear shift away from schemes to support traditional, declining sectors and a shift of resources towards new generation and high technology activities in particular. In some cases, this move is associated with the development of more horizontal schemes designed to stimulate the use of particular technologies or processes in general, rather than with the introduction of new sector–specific schemes. Apart from efforts to improve the general business climate, incentives measures have also been used to stimulate collaborative research, focusing on priority sectors or technologies, and to improve the availability of risk capital. In general it appears that greater efforts are being devoted to policy delivery.

Certain of the above developments, particularly those focusing on the use of new technologies and policy delivery, have also been important elements of Member countries' policies directed at stimulating the growth and development of small firms. While policy in this area has sometimes been associated with the introduction of new incentives or the creation of differentials in favour of small firms, the main thrust of incentives policies has been to open up existing measures to these firms where they were previously not eligible and, more particularly, to increase the awareness of small firms of the existence and relevance of available incentives. In addition, a development of note has been the expansion of non–financial assistance to small enterprises in the form of the provision of consultancy and other business services.

The services sector represents a further area where there have been important developments over the last years. Similar to the approach for small enterprises, enterprises in the services sector increasingly benefit from investment incentives. The previous approach typical of many countries, whereas specific service sector incentives were operated is being replaced by the opening up of more general investment incentives schemes to specified services activities. Employment intensive services benefit from the job–related aspects of these schemes, while those which are more capital intensive benefit from the extension of previously manufacturing orientated schemes. In a number of cases more intangible aspects, such as patenting and licensing, are also eligible for incentives.

Somewhat less emphasis is being given to regional policy in recent years, yet almost all Member countries continue to give this area a relatively high priority. In a number of countries there have been important cut–backs in expenditure on regional assistance and a contraction in spatial coverage. There have been moves within regional incentives to stimulate new areas of growth and importance, particularly high technology activities, producer services and small firms, and, more generally, to improve the general business environment in the problem regions. Regional incentives have also witnessed some change in emphasis from automatic to discretionary award schemes and a decentralisation of policy delivery, associated with the more general themes of improving policy delivery, productivity and value for money.

Trends in the use of disincentives in the OECD area are more difficult to identify, in part because a number of the disincentives discussed in this report were not surveyed in the 1983 study. What can be expected, however, is some tendency towards reduction in their scope and application. This would certainly be expected from the need to promote investment given the present low growth environment and the greater reliance on market forces to direct investment. Indeed, it seems that many Member countries may now be devoting greater emphasis to attracting international direct investment by a removal or reduction of restrictions, impediments and other disincentive measures. As concerns trade–related investment measures, there is a clear trend towards their limitation in the OECD area in comparison to the early eighties, which is associated with the more general trend in Member countries to liberalise their policy regimes towards international investment. The same appears to be true in some developing countries, which have relaxed or removed trade–related investment measures, but in other developing countries there seems to be little movement in respect of these measures; indeed, in some cases, new or stricter measures have been reported.

Section 1.   SCOPE OF THE MEASURES ADDRESSED

At the outset of this work it is necessary to face the difficult task of establishing a definition of the concepts of "investment incentives and disincentives" as these concepts often vary according to the context in which they are used. The main concern is to avoid any rigid or arbitrary definition which would unduly restrict the scope of the survey and prejudge further analyses based on it. Consequently, a flexible approach capable of accommodating a wide range of measures that are of interest for the purposes of the study, and in particular that may be most relevant to the international investment process, is adopted. Rather broad definitions of the terms "incentives" and "disincentives" are used but the scope of the survey has been demarcated more precisely by means of pragmatic criteria.

Specifically, the survey is based on the following definition of international investment incentives: an incentive will be understood as any government measure designed to influence an investment decision, or having the effect of increasing the profit accruing to the potential investment or altering the risks attached to it. This definition includes measures which may lead a potential investor to modify a project, even if these measures do not influence directly the profitability of the project as long as they affect the risk involved. It has the advantage of excluding economic factors such as market size, comparative advantage and price stability, or socio–political factors which determine the general context or climate of investment and corresponding general policies. However, it is stressed that the necessary distinction between the measures included in the survey and economic or socio–political factors presents certain difficulties. For instance, measures reducing the rate of taxes on profits in specific sectors in a particular country are to be considered as investment incentives even though the reduced tax rate may be higher than the general rate of taxes on profits in another country. More generally, investment incentive measures are sometimes taken with the purpose of compensating for what are considered as unfavourable influences of economic and socio–political factors. These elements have to be kept in mind, and obviously the role of economic or socio–political factors, which may carry considerable weight in an investment decision, are to be taken into consideration in further analyses, for instance, when assessing the impact and effectiveness of the measures singled out in accordance with the definition used. Disincentives to international direct investment will be understood as any government measures which are designed to or which have the effect of reducing the profit accruing to the investment or increasing the risks attached to it. While certain measures are clearly taken to limit or exclude investment, particularly foreign direct investment, in particular sectors or activities, others are intended to ensure the achievement of particular goals or objectives, although these measures may clearly have a disincentive or discouragement effect on investment.

As investment incentives and disincentives raise complex issues cutting across major aspects of domestic as well as international investment, a certain amount of overlap of this work programme on incentives and disincentives with work done elsewhere, within and outside the OECD, is unavoidable. The primary objective is to promote transparency in this field. However, to avoid undesirable duplication of efforts and to reduce the scope of the survey in order to make it more specific and operational, some additional categories of measures referred to in the paragraphs below have been excluded from the present survey. Some such measures may nevertheless be discussed occasionally in this report when, for example, it is felt that they are of particular relevance or when the Member country concerned has itself reported such a measure as an important component of its incentives and disincentives programmes.

Disincentives attached to the authorisation of inward direct investment and/or establishment, including pre–conditions or performance requirements linked to authorisation of inward direct investment, are excluded from the survey as they are under the surveillance of the Committee on Capital Movements and Invisible Transactions, which is responsible for overseeing the application of the Code of Liberalisation of Capital Movements. A survey of such measures, recently published by the OECD, is to be found in "Controls and Impediments Affecting Inward Investment in Member Countries", which updates a 1981 study on that topic. Similarly, obstacles, restrictions or impediments related to investments by foreign–controlled enterprises already established in the host country are generally excluded (these being dealt with by the Committee on International Investment and Multinational Enterprises in its work on the National Treatment instrument), except where they relate specifically to the incentives and disincentives listed in the typology presented below. Thus, for example, specific mention would be made when there is discriminatory treatment of established foreign–controlled enterprises with respect to the fiscal, financial or other incentives offered by governments or where, for example, restrictions relating to equity participation are placed on investments by such enterprises. A full survey of such measures is found in the 1986 OECD publication *National Treatment for Enterprises under Foreign Control.*

The survey also seeks to avoid undesirable overlap with work conducted elsewhere concerning traditional export subsidies. The main purpose of these subsidies lies in the field of trade policy, although in some cases they may have an effect on investment. Furthermore, these measures are subject to specific rules and procedures prescribed by the above–mentioned GATT Code of Subsidies qnd Countervailing Duties. They are not included in the survey, on the understanding that the possible repercussions on investment of these measures should be part of a complete economic assessment of incentives and disincentives. However, a number of incentives to international investment may be seen as also affecting trade flows, some of these possibly leading to trade distortion. In this sense, the measures in question may be considered as trade–related investment incentive measures. These measures are covered in this report as well as trade–related investment measures which are likely to have disincentive effects on investment.

Finally, home country incentives to outward investment which, for the most part, concern investments directed towards developing countries, are also excluded from the survey as they are documented in the OECD publication, "Investing in Developing Countries", OECD, 1983 (which is currently being updated) although a few remarks are made in respect of these measures.

Thus, the present survey focuses principally on the following measures taken at the national, and where appropriate, sub–national levels applied to investments within the OECD area.

a) Measures taken by host countries:

    i) Investment incentives, subdivided into:
- fiscal measures (such as accelerated depreciation, preferential tax rates, tax exemptions and tax credits, and including also measures relating to social security contributions and investment reserves);
- financial measures (such as grants, preferential loans and loan guarantees);
- other, non–financial, measures (including certain infrastructure–related assistance, preferential government contracts, the provision of certain services, and the establishment of free–trade, enterprise and technology zones);

    ii) Disincentives, including:
- trade–related investment measures which have disincentive effects and other disincentives and conditions linked to incentive awards;

b) Measures affecting outward investment.

Two further points need to be made to clarify the scope of the survey. First, while no clean cut delineation based on the distinction between specific investment incentive measures and macroeconomic incentives measures (such as temporary measures taken by governments to revive demand for capital goods, subsidies to imports of raw materials, or even exchange rate policies) can be made, the latter remain largely outside the scope of the survey, bearing in mind not only the nature but also the objective of an incentive measure. Secondly, government measures to improve infrastructure (e.g. transport, telephone networks) are excluded from the survey, except if these measures are taken with the explicit aim of attracting investment (for example, in certain cases, the creation of industrial zones). On the other hand, general aids to enterprises in the form, say, of tax reliefs granted under structural or regional policies fall within the scope of the survey.

In a number of important areas, the scope of the present survey parallels that taken in the OECD 1983 publication on this subject. Efforts have been made in this survey, however, to cover a number of lacunae identified in that publication meriting future study including, in particular, trade–related investment measures, some categories of preconditions and performance requirements measures taken by home countries and measures taken at sub–national levels.

Section 2. OBJECTIVES AND INSTRUMENTS OF INCENTIVES AND DISINCENTIVES POLICIES

a) **Policy objectives**

The general economic philosophy underlying Member countries' approaches to stimulating the level, nature and location of investment is one based on promoting and facilitating the role of market forces. While there are, of course, important differences in the positions of Member countries, a common approach has been to establish an environment of confidence and stability through the use of macroeconomic fiscal and monetary policies, and to use microeconomic measures, including investment incentives to reinforce the operation of market forces, and to foster the changes required by new patterns of demand and supply. This is also reflected in their approaches to industrial or regional policies, which define the context for a number of specific investment programmes in many Member countries.

The main objectives to which the investment incentive measures examined in this study are addressed fall into a number of broad categories. A first main objective is that of *industrial policy*, which may encompass general, industry–wide objectives, such as structural adjustment or greater productivity and efficiency, or may be addressed to particular sectors (for example, those experiencing high levels of international competition but also new, dynamic high technology areas) or groups of enterprises (such as small firms) and can also refer to the promotion of R&D and the application of advanced technologies. In some countries, science and technology forms part and parcel of industrial policy while in others, it would appear to be a more separate policy area.

While all Member countries pursue investment incentives policies geared to industrial objectives, there are often important differences in their positions and priorities. In general, the main approach to stimulating investment is by the use of macroeconomic policies geared to improve the overall economic climate and strengthen the operation of market forces, with varying degrees of reliance on government intervention and involvement or use of microeconomic and incentives measures. Broadly speaking, Member countries' policies in the field of industry and technology, as in other areas, have moved from defensive to positive approaches, seeking less to support declining industries and diverting more resources towards growth and high technology areas. Some approaches have been redefined to operate more in harmony with market mechanisms and promoting more generally an economic climate more conducive to stimulating changes dictated by developments in the competitive situation. This change in emphasis has been quite definite and marked in a large number of countries.

Within these general redirections or reorientations in policies aimed at structural adaptation (which are discussed in more detail in Section 3), Member countries rely principally on setting the broad economic framework within which such adjustments take place, supplementing this to varying degrees by measures more specifically addressed to pointing to desired directions of change and accelerating the implementation of changes in such directions. In other cases, measures are pursued, particularly in respect of the more traditional sectors, with a view to managing the pace and conditions of change to ensure orderly adjustment. A number of countries therefore have sectoral schemes geared to the continuing difficulties faced by and adjustments required in sectors such as shipbuilding, steel and textiles, although in a number of instances, previous sector specific measures have been brought to an end. Particularly noteworthy is that a number of countries have introduced schemes specific to particular advanced activities such as aerospace, robotics, optical fibres, computers and software.

Measures designed to correct *regional imbalances* continue to play an important and sometimes a major role. In the past, regional measures tended to focus on the manufacturing sector and on the relocation of mobile industry to the assisted regions. Also the tendency, already observed for some time now, has continued whereby greater emphasis is being placed on mobilising the indigenous potential of the assisted regions, focusing on enterprises already established in these areas, including also small and medium sized enterprises and certain parts of the services sector. Also, greater emphasis is being given to changing often outdated industrial structures via the promotion of activities using advanced technology.

If certain developments in the field of incentives related to industrial policy can be characterised by a shift of emphasis from traditional, declining industries to expanding, technology–intensive activities, some developments in the field of regional policy measures are often more characterised by reduced levels of intervention. However, and despite the fact that regional policies have tended to go down the priority listings in recent years for a variety of reasons (including high levels of unemployment nationwide) it is interesting that most countries still include regional development among their main objectives. This being said, the experiences of countries have differed over the last years. For example, in quite a number of countries regional policy objectives still maintain high levels of importance (e.g., Italy, Norway, Sweden) whereas in other countries, at least at the national level, they are of a much lower significance (e.g., United States and Australia, but perhaps because of the importance of measures at the sub–national level in these countries). In other cases, particularly Denmark, France and the United Kingdom there have been important cutbacks in expenditure and/or the areas in which regional incentives apply. As in other broad areas of policy, regional policy has experienced significant cause for reflection and the move from "defensive" to "positive" approaches has been an important feature of the discussion. In a number of instances therefore, regional policy measures have been significantly reorientated, and in cases noticeably reduced. This is not because the problem itself has been reduced, but rather that the context of the problems and solutions which have characterised discussion have changed, often quite profoundly. Examples of such changes, which will be discussed in more detail in Section 3, include the abolition or reduction in the value of certain measures, reductions in the areas covered by such measures and redirections to include or place more focus on aspects such as services, indigenous industry and small firms.

Recent years have also seen the introduction or strengthening of investment incentive measures related to more specific targets. A particular example is that of measures geared to *small and medium–sized enterprises*. The rationale underlying these measures stems from the growing recognition of the role of small and medium sized enterprises in the industrial fabric of a region or a country, and their contribution to technology and employment. While there are certainly examples of measures introduced specifically for small enterprises or where differentials in their favour have been created or where thresholds have been lowered to allow their inclusion in schemes, the basic thrust of the approach in this area has been on advising smaller enterprises that they are eligible for existing measures. Greater efforts on policy delivery are reflected, inter alia, in the devolution or decentralisation of policy administration, with for example regional and technology transfer policies being delivered by agencies and organisations throughout a country. Another facet of the approach involves attempts in many countries to ease new company formation, including the encouragement of venture capital activities and various business expansion schemes. More generally, moves to improve the general economic climate for business, as noted above, can also be expected to benefit small enterprises. Similarly, although much less widespread, note can be taken of measures geared to energy conservation and environmental improvement.

Sustained high levels of *unemployment* constitute a major problem in many Member countries. The main policies pursued to promote employment are macroeconomic in nature. In addition there are specific schemes aimed at particular disadvantaged groups (especially the young and the long–term unemployed) training schemes and schemes which aim to improve occupational and regional mobility, to provide work experience and so on. These various measures fall outside the scope of the present report. This being said, a policy objective underlying many investment incentives measures is to support employment either by creating jobs or at least maintaining or securing existing jobs. In some cases, this will be an indirect effect dependent on the level and nature of investment stimulated by the measures. In other cases, it will arise through the use of minimum employment requirements associated with the award of incentives or other job–related aspects in the evaluation of applications for incentives. There are, for example, a number of measures explicitly assisting employment, for example, via training grants or by offering higher levels of award dependent on the number of jobs created.

As noted in Section 1 above, certain measures concerning or defined in relation to *trade objectives* are also covered in this study. While most OECD countries rely on industrial, regional and other policy areas to stimulate output, investment, employment and exports, trade objectives may nevertheless be included in the goals of incentives policies. Furthermore trade–related aspects may be included in the conditions associated with the award of incentives. It is also worthwhile mentioning that in some countries (particularly Australia) such trade–related measures are seen as important components of overall policy. In other instances, for example in Ireland, measures explicitly designed to promote exports were replaced in 1981 by more general measures geared, in the first instance, to investment.

Some of the *disincentive measures* addressed in this report are also geared to trade–related objectives, for example, local content or export requirements. More generally, however, the disincentive measures included in the present study, which as noted above are much more frequently used in developing countries as compared to the OECD area, may also be taken for a variety of other reasons including protecting the domestic sector, securing host country benefits from inward direct investment or counteracting what some host countries perceive as practices of multinational enterprises which would reduce the scale of such benefits. For example, local content requirements may be used to stimulate activity in the domestic sector or with a view to improving the integration of foreign–controlled enterprises into the host country economy. Other measures which may have disincentive effects, such as local equity or R&D requirements, may be based on similar motivations, for example when R&D requirements are used to ensure a given degree of technological capacity in the foreign–controlled subsidiary.

Conditions associated with the award of incentives are typically related to defining the eligibility of projects for awards under particular schemes and to concerns with viability and incrementality, i.e., to ensure that assistance is provided to projects which will be viable and to projects demonstrating a real need for assistance. In addition to these, other conditions may be associated with, for example, the creation or maintenance of employment or, as noted above, with trade–related goals. While such conditions can therefore be traced to reasons concerning the accountability of public expenditure and to ensuring value and real benefits from the use of public monies, it is also the case that many of the preconditions or performance requirements referred to in the paragraph above, are, in OECD Member countries, set out as conditions to investment incentive awards and the benefits to the host country thereby expected are considered as a justification of such awards.

In the course of the Committee's discussion, the question was raised as to whether measures which affect the exports of foreign located affiliates of domestic companies could have a disincentive effect on outward investment. Where such measures exist, they may be linked to balance–of–payments goals, taken to protect particular domestic industries (for example, when foreign production might lower the quality of the product), to prevent the export of employment or particular skills or techniques or in relation to foreign policy or national security motivations.

b)   Policy instruments

Member countries continue to use a wide variety of instruments in pursuing the objectives set for their incentives policies. While there have been noticeable changes in the emphasis or orientation of particular policies in Member countries, it seems that there have not been fundamental changes in the armoury of measures used by governments. There have certainly been a number of occasions where particular measures have been abolished and replaced by others or where entirely new measures have been introduced, yet it seems that the main response with respect to actual instruments has been to keep more or less the same types of measures, but adapt them to new situations, for example, via streamling targetting or changes in applicability, eligibility and levels and conditions of award. Below, the positions and patterns with respect to these measures are described briefly and following the typology set out in Section 1 above. The discussion, therefore, focuses first on incentives at the national level (fiscal, financial and non–financial measures) and subsequently at sub–national levels. Following this, trade–related and other disincentive measures, conditions associated with the award of incentives and measures affecting outward investment are examined.

Investment incentives

— Fiscal incentives

Obviously, and before discussing specific types of fiscal incentives, the broad fiscal régime in a country, particularly the rate of corporation tax, has a major bearing on investment, and general reductions in the rate of corporation tax will clearly provide investment with an important incentive. Over the last years, many Member countries have been modifying their fiscal policies to improve the general environment for investment, for example, and most recently, in the United States where a very comprehensive reform is being undertaken. In Canada, changes in the corporate income tax system took place in 1985 revealing changes in the philosophy underlying corporate tax policy. These changes took the form of a more results–based tax system, featuring broader based incentives provided through lower tax rates and the elimination or reduction of selective, up–front deductions and credits. These changes were designed with the objective of having a less complex tax system and one which would interfere less with business decisions, leaving these to be determined more by business rather than tax considerations.

Specific fiscal incentives of various types and characteristics are operated by all Member countries in the broad policy areas discussed above. The main types of fiscal measures include accelerated depreciation and various forms of preferential tax treatment such as reductions, exemptions and credits, while in a fewer number of cases, reductions in social security contributions (as in Italy, for example) or tax free investment reserves (as in Sweden, for example) are also found. It can also be noted that in one or two countries, various forms of fiscal incentives are offered, it being left to the applicant to decide which particular form is most appropriate to his needs (for example, as in Austria). In the same vein, in Germany, such a choice also exists between a tax concession and a financial grant but for practical purposes, the award is nearly always paid as a grant.

Generally, there are fewer fiscal incentives than financial incentives (although countries such as Australia and the United States represent exceptions to this general pattern). This, of course, says nothing about the respective values of given fiscal and financial awards and, in any event, the general fiscal régime is a very important element in countries' overall approach to stimulating investment.

Fiscal measures tend to be very general in nature, aiming to stimulate investment across the board, whereas financial incentives normally focus on a narrower policy objective, for example to stimulate regional development, encourage R&D, help small firms etc. Amongst other things, this is due to the fact that fiscal measures are generally the responsibility of the tax authorities whereas financial incentives are administered directly by those responsible for the policy area in question. However, a number of fiscal incentives do focus on particular investment activities, most commonly research, but also in some cases the problem regions, particular sectors (especially mining), energy saving and environmental protection. In recent years, an interesting development in a number of countries such as Australia, Austria, Ireland, Norway and the United Kingdom has been the award of fiscal concessions to encourage equity funding of new, often high risk, business start–ups.

By far the most common fiscal incentive measure is the accelerated depreciation allowance. There are, however, other incentives types worth mentioning. For example, Ireland offers low (10 per cent) levels of corporation tax for profits arising from the sale of manufactured goods, replacing in 1981 the system of export sales relief, and similarly the United Kingdom has also recently replaced accelerated depreciation by lower corporation tax schedules. The investment account (WIR) in the Netherlands is also interesting, especially since it has been recently evaluated and found to be superior to other measures analysed such as accelerated depreciation or investment allowances.

— Financial incentives

Financial incentives take the main forms of grants, various types of concessional financing such as loans at preferential rates and loan guarantees. Most countries operate one and sometimes several financial measures addressed to the main broad areas of incentives policies. However, the bulk of financial measures tend to address specific policy areas where their discretionary aspects permit the required targetting, where the main targets for financial incentives are regional development, R&D and small firms. In addition, sectoral development, structural adaptation, energy saving and environmental protection are other targets for financial incentives, mainly in the form of grants.

In the area of regional policy and while most countries offer a package of measures, capital grants form the mainstay of most assistance packages, although other financial incentives, such as interest subsidies, preferential loans, loan guarantees, training grants and other job—related grants are also found. The importance of capital grants in regional policies reflects their relative ease of administration, their visibility and the consideration that they provide a direct subsidy in an area where financial subsidy is felt to be essential to stimulating investment and location.

Grants and technical development loans are the main types of financial incentives directed at stimulating R&D. In a number of countries, there are provisions for grants to be repaid if the supported project is successful, for example in countries such as Denmark and the Netherlands where loans become non—repayable should the project fail. This repayable feature of grants and loans is linked to the fact that R&D is often a high risk area requiring also relatively high levels of subsidy. Administrations are therefore likely to be in a position to offer more money if they expect to get most of it back. Financial awards to small firms generally take the form of loans and loan guarantees as the availability of finance is often more of a bottleneck for such firms than is access to a subsidy.

While, as noted above, measures to stimulate risk capital formation are typically fiscal in nature, some financial measures are also addressed to this objective. In recent years a number of governments or public agencies have taken, generally temporary, equity stakes in investments in high risk areas (as opposed to loss—making situations) generally via regional development agencies as in Italy and the United Kingdom or through venture capital companies operating nationwide, as in the Netherlands.

— Non—financial measures

All Member countries offer at least one and usually several non—financial measures. These generally comprise two main groups of measures with the first set, comprising the provision of infrastructure and business services, found in just about every country while the second group, which covers government purchasing and the use of export, enterprise and technology zones, is generally less widespread.

The provision of certain infrastructural investment such as prepared industrial sites and the construction of factories in anticipation of occupation (advance factories), is often used in the context of regional policy, but also in urban policy in a number of countries. In comparison to the provision of traditional infrastructure of these types, which is a well established approach, many countries have been developing in recent years a new type of business infrastructure, namely the provision of information, consultancy and management services as well as training and other technical assistance often focused on small firms, technology transfer and/or regional problem areas. The development of business services infrastructure is frequently seen as a key component of government policies in these areas.

A number of countries such as Australia, Italy and Norway use government purchasing to pursue particular objectives such as regional development, and government procurement policies also appear to be of major importance in the United States at the sub-national level.

Customs free zones (or export processing zones), enterprise zones and science parks represent another component of non-financial measures. Customs free zones or freeports are found in a number of countries such as Austria, Ireland, Germany, Spain and the United Kingdom, where the exemption from customs duties is directed, inter alia, to stimulating processing industries. While by no means a new component of policy, it does seem that the number of such zones has been expanding recently. By comparison, science parks and enterprise zones are relatively new forms of non-financial measures and seem to be of growing importance, both in numbers of zones and numbers of countries introducing these zones. Enterprise zones, which offer relaxed or streamlined beaurocratic control and the removal of certain fiscal burdens, are perhaps the most recent development, with such zones being set up in Belgium, France and the United Kingdom in the last years. In general terms, zones of all three types tend to fall outside the sphere of traditional policy fields such as regional or inner city policies, although there are exceptions such as the Shannon free zone in Ireland which is more closely tied to regional policy.

— Incentives at sub-national levels

The investment incentives programmes discussed in this report are financed or administered at various levels of government — national, state, regional, local and municipal. In many countries, incentives programmes are predominantly central government programmes, but to varying degrees such measures are found at the sub-national level in these countries. Equally, situations where sub-national systems are dominant are few with probably only the United States, falling into this category, while in other countries, there are varying degrees of shared responsibilities with Canada, Germany, Switzerland, providing the best examples. Obviously, the relative importance of national versus sub-national measures is a reflection of institutional structures in countries which range from the federal or confederal to more centralised patterns. Evolution in such patterns tends to be slow as institutional structures are usually defined in a legal, and often constitutional manner.

However, in the area of regional policy at least, and while policy formulation is still very much a central responsibility, the delivery of policy is increasingly being entrusted to the sub-national level. As the examples of the following paragraphs reveal, however, the extent of sub-national authority covers a spectrum ranging from the regionalisation of policy administration, through the regional decision making authority for projects up to a certain size, to the devolution of budgets.

In a large number of countries including Australia, Austria, Denmark, Ireland, Japan, the Netherlands, Norway, and the United Kingdom, measures by the central level are dominant; indeed in Ireland, Japan and Norway, for example, there are very few or only minor schemes at sub–national levels. The situation with respect to sub–national measures varies with respect to their importance in the overall system of awards. For example, in Australia, measures promoting regional development are primarily the responsibility of the individual states, while in Belgium, and although the main measures are financed centrally, the application of measures related to the Economic Expansion Acts, as well as measures for small and medium–sized enterprises falls within the competence of the regional authorities. In the Netherlands, sub–national measures are generally ad hoc, incidental and minor, but the provincial authorities now deal with applications for smaller levels of awards within national schemes. Similarly in Norway, where only transport subsidies are operated at the sub–national level, decisions concerning projects qualifying for regional assistance are increasingly taken at the county level. Local authorities in the United Kingdom play a minor role in providing assistance and their powers are closely circumscribed by central government. Although the level of provision varies in intensity and type, it is mainly for small businesses.

In a number of other countries, there is a more even distribution of measures between central and sub–national levels of government. In Germany, and although the most important incentives are measures at the federal level, the main regional policy investment measure, the investment allowance, is jointly administered by the federal and state authorities who also broadly share the cost of foregone tax revenues. In contrast, R&D is primarily (but not exclusively) a federal responsibility and small firm development is mainly entrusted to the states. As in Germany, some investment programmes in Austria are administered jointly by the federal and provincial governments.

In Canada, regional development activities inevitably involve many objectives and requirements on which the federal and provincial governments must agree before priorities on joint actions can be established. Since 1983, federal–provincial interaction has taken the form of Economic and Regional Development Agreements (ERDA), which are ten–year agreements between the government of Canada and individual provinces. These agreements identify priorities shared by federal and provincial governments which form the basis for co–ordinated action by the federal and provincial governments through ERDA sub–agreements. These sub–agreements are formal contracts between the federal and provincial governments which define specific programmes or projects which both levels of government will undertake in specific areas such as transportation, agriculture, etc. As concerns investment incentives to business, the Canadian provincial governments, in an effort to attract new investment and industry, have developed a range of programmes to provide professional, technical and financial services. In addition, several provinces have created economic development corporations which offer financial assistance in the form of subsidies, loan guarantees and participation in share capital.

The relative importance of sub–national vis–à–vis national measures appears to be highest in the United States, where the federal government has traditionally relied on general macroeconomic policies rather than specific incentives to stimulate business. Apart from the investment tax credit, federal incentives programmes are generally of a relatively limited nature. By comparison, incentives programmes offered by the states and localities appear to be much more important, although quantitative comparisons are not available. Federal-state co-operation mechanisms, in areas relating for example to regional development, is not with individual states but with multi-state commissions and targetting to regions and areas in economic distress is frequently done as a federal-local partnership. In Switzerland, there are federal programmes which, although traditionally restricted in time, scope and extent, have progressively expanded over the years. However, policy is chiefly the responsibility of cantons. Incentives at the cantonal level are stronger than those at the federal level.

While a number of fiscal incentives exist at sub-national levels in countries such as Canada, Switzerland and the United States, this form of incentive is much less predominant than financial or non-financial measures. To some extent this feature will depend also on the extent to which sub-national levels have fiscal authority and, even here, questions relating to cost (i.e. foregone fiscal revenue) are likely to be important determinants of the form of assistance. This is also reflected in the composition of financial awards, where there are relatively few grant systems, with most measures taking the form of loan credits or guarantees.

Some sub-national fiscal measures are found, for example, at the provincial level in Canada, at the cantonal level in Switzerland and by the states in the United States. In Canada, Nova Scotia and Quebec offer tax incentives in the form of R&D credits. In Switzerland, a number of cantons grant special tax treatment to holding companies (e.g. capital and reserves taxes assessed at a reduced rate). Commercial, industrial and service companies are often offered certain tax incentives to encourage location in their cantons such as relief on cantonal or municipal taxes, including in some cases tax exemptions for a protracted period or accelerated depreciation. In the United States, most states offer tax incentives to encourage business development, typically by refraining from levying a particular tax or by partial reductions in taxes related to corporate income, sales and use taxes and/or property taxes. Examples of such measures commonly found at the state level include exemptions from sales and uses taxes on the purchase of plant and equipment, exemptions related to goods in transit in interstate commerce and exemptions from property taxes for business inventories. Also, in most states, tax credits are offered on corporate income tax for the creation of jobs or investment and in some cases, particular investments may be promoted via targetting of these measures.

As noted above, financial incentives at sub-national levels are used much more frequently, with the notable exception of grants. Variable but significant levels of provision are found in countries such as Australia, Austria, Canada, Germany, Switzerland and the United States. As with their national level counterparts, the main types of such measures fall into two broad groups — loans and loan guarantees and subsidising site costs and other infrastructure provision. To a lesser extent, grants and measures aimed at improving the availability of finance are also found.

Concessional finance through cheaper loans is found in countries such as Australia (with respect to the purchase of sites), Austria via reduced rates of interest, Switzerland via subsidies to interest rates and the United States. In the latter, firms may have access to subsidised state loans, although the principle form is that of industrial revenue bonds. These bonds, offered by public authorities or agencies are found in most states. The interest received by lenders is not subject to federal income tax thus permitting lower interest rates and thereby providing an interest subsidy to the borrower. Other forms of equity financing found at the state level, although much less common, include umbrella bonds which are composite bonds providing for the financing of a number of small investments when individual investments are so small that the cost of bond issue is prohibitive relative to the required capital. Umbrella bonds may also be used to finance firms whose credit rating is not sufficient to qualify for industrial revenue bond financing. General obligation bonds are less common, as they are backed by the issuing authority. Approval procedures are therefore much more stringent, and such bonds are generally limited to financing local infrastructure investments.

Loan guarantees are offered at the sub–national level in Australia, Austria, Canada, Germany, Switzerland, the United States. By guaranteeing the debt or part of the debt of particular investments such as those of high risk, innovative ventures or by small enterprises, the risk premium is reduced or eliminated permitting the firm to borrow at below market levels of interest rates. Another form of financial assistance, though less frequently found concerns the provision of finance (often at non–subsidised rates) whereby the body providing the finance may act as a lender of last resort. Some of the state loans available in the United States have this feature, whereby firms applying for loans must demonstrate that financing is not available from conventional sources or is so only at prohibitive interest rates. Another source of funding sometimes found is development credit corporations or other such bodies providing risk capital. These bodies are often privately organised and generate significant proportions of their lending capital from private sources. Most frequently, they provide relatively small loans for working capital at above prime interest rates.

Non–financial measures are also available at the sub–national level in a number of countries such as Austria, Canada, Germany, the Netherlands, Switzerland, the United Kingdom and the United States, although the types of measures offered as well as their intensity can vary significantly. The main types of such measures, similar to those often found at the national level, include the provision of specific infrastructure, sites and premises, the creation of enterprise zones and the provision of services, technical assistance and training programmes.

Disincentives and conditions attached to incentives

This section discusses measures which may have a disincentive effect on investment, particularly international direct investment. It addresses, firstly, trade–related and other disincentive measures in the OECD area and secondly, other conditions associated with incentives awards. Following that, trade–related and other disincentives in developing countries are considered. Trade–related investment incentives are not discussed in the present section which focuses on the disincentive effects of measures.

— Trade–related and other disincentive measures in OECD countries

A variety of measures may have a disincentive effect on investment from abroad. These include: local content requirements, export requirements, trade–balancing requirements, product mandating requirements, technology transfer requirements, local equity requirements, exchange and remittance restrictions, manufacturing requirements or limitations, and various other restrictions and requirements concerning, for example, financing, the modality of the investment or investment into unrelated areas.

Obviously, many of these measures can be seen as trade–related investment measures, as they do also appear to have an impact on trade flows, this being especially the case for the first ones listed in the above paragraph, where their impact on trade flows appears to be intentional and quite direct.

The types of measures listed above may be linked to the award of incentives (for example, the availability or level of a particular award may be conditional upon or in some way proportional to the fulfilment of such requirements or may enter more generally into the assessment of applications for incentives) but in other cases they may be separate from incentives systems. For example, they may arise as a condition imposed at the time of establishment, acquisition or expansion of a direct foreign investment or they may be created when an investor commits to undertake certain activities as a result of negotiations with government authorities concerning the terms under which the investment will take place. Although the topic of differential treatment of domestic and foreign–controlled enterprises within incentives systems is discussed below, it can be pointed out at the present juncture that while the use of such measures as conditions on establishment, acquisition or expansion is generally restricted to investments of foreign–controlled enterprises, in other situations they may apply to both domestic and foreign–controlled enterprises. Even here, however, there may be discriminatory treatment; for example, certain types of incentives measures may be reserved only to domestic enterprises or requirements at higher levels may be imposed on foreign–controlled enterprises.

On the basis of the information collected for the present study, four countries (Australia, Denmark, Norway and the United Kingdom) maintain trade–related or other disincentive measures, or at least have particular policies which may involve, in certain circumstances, elements of such measures. For example, in Austria local content requirements are not imposed as a prerequesite for investment promotion, but local content declarations by enterprises can be considered as good–will declarations. The majority of such requirements concerns local content, typically with respect to particular sectors. Local content requirements are found in the automobile and components sector in Australia (while Ireland has recently dropped such a measure), in relation to tobacco and minerals processing in Australia and in oil–related activities in Denmark, Norway and the United Kingdom. The latter group of measures, which relates to bidding procedures, has the objective of generally ensuring that local producers have a full and fair opportunity to compete. Normally, such full and fair opportunity policies do not require companies to meet specific preconditions or performance requirements or to make particular commitments, other than to give full and fair opportunity to domestic suppliers to tender for contracts with a view to developing the domestic sector. In the Norwegian case, however, domestic goods and services which are competitive must be used. Whereas the above local content requirements are specific to individual sectors, that in Australia related to government purchases is more general in application.

In the United Kingdom, in the area of mergers legislation, certain assurances, which could be trade–related, may be sought or accepted before a given merger may proceed. It should be noted, however, that such assurances are sought only infrequently and exceptionally.

Other measures, which may have disincentive effects on investment (particularly inward investment) concern requirements stipulating local equity holding (i.e., domestic ownership levels) and requirements related to the level, nature or location of R&D activities or facilities. Such measures are found in five countries (Australia, Japan, Norway, Switzerland and the United States). All of these countries have local equity requirements concerning, generally, key sectors such as broadcasting (Australia, Japan), telecommunications (Australia, Japan, and the United States), oil and nuclear power-related activities (Switzerland), the maritime sector (Austria — registration of ships) and financial services (Norway). In addition, Austria has performance requirements related to R&D expenditure.

In addition to the measures addressed above, a number of countries also have measures with possible disincentive effects related to the award of discretionary incentives. In some cases, a given award or the amount of the award may be conditional on the agreement of a particular performance requirement. In other cases, aspects such as imports, exports, marketing arrangements and technology transfer may enter into the general assessment of applications for incentives awards. While little information on the latter practice is available it is likely that, to varying extents, many Member countries examine such features in assessing applications for awards.

Finally, it is also interesting at this point to mention the National Linkage Programme in Ireland. This programme was introduced in 1986 in order to develop linkages between larger, export-orientated firms and potential suppliers with a view to increasing, inter alia, the integration of foreign-controlled operations into the domestic economy and stimulating the growth of domestic enterprises. The programme, which is therefore aimed at matching the output of small firms with the requirements of multinational enterprises in Ireland imposes no legal requirements on companies, but is nevertheless aimed at improving local content.

— Other conditions associated with incentives awards in OECD countries

Investment incentives invariably have conditions of award attached to them. Three groups of such conditions can be identified; firstly, conditions relating to scheme objectives (e.g. to undertake investment, locate in problem regions etc.); secondly, conditions relating to the project's chance of success or viability or to the impact of the incentives (i.e., that they make something happen that would not have otherwise); and finally, other conditions not directly related to the scheme's main objective (e.g. employment conditions). The latter two categories apply only to discretionary schemes.

The first set of conditions is self-evident and part and parcel of the nature of incentives policies. Investment incentive programmes are generally geared to specific objectives and it is therefore natural that the measures associated with these programmes are applied only if investment does contribute to these objectives. For instance, incentive programmes specific to new investment generally require that new investment actually occurs, and incentive programmes designed to favour the location of investment in particular regions are restricted to investment actually taking place in these regions.

A second set of conditions is associated with the efficient use and accountability of expenditure on investment incentives. Such requirements include the need for projects to display viability (i.e. that they have a sound chance of commercial success) and that they also display a need for assistance, i.e. that incentives are not used to assist investments that would have been realised anyway in the absence of assistance. The growing prevalence of and emphasis given to such viability and additionality criteria may be traced to a number of factors including tight budgetary situations, the move from "defensive" to positive measures placing priority on promising, high risk and innovative investments, as well as a certain disappointment with the benefits that have resulted from a number of investment incentive programmes.

The above types of conditions, eligibility, viability, and additionality generally form the main components of the review of investment projects with respect to their entitlement to incentives. The general objectives of such reviews are to ensure that public funds are spent in an accountable manner and to ensure value for monies spent. Thus, for example, net economic benefit to the country (within which certain, usually large foreign investments are also reviewed), is an element of the Canadian assessment of applications for assistance.

Somewhat apart from the types of conditions described above, some incentives programmes involve specific preconditions or performance requirements which are not related in a straightforward manner to the main objectives of the programmes. An example of such requirements are those related to employment. In Europe, and with respect to regional policy, countries such as Austria and France stipulate minimum job conditions in respect of setting up projects. In other cases, conditions may relate more to the maintenance of employment or to training. In general, employment and related conditions are seldom found outside the regional policy area, and even here not all countries apply such conditions. In any event, it would seem that the emphasis on job creation or maintenance in investment incentives is less than it was in the past. In the case of some countries, this is associated with the move from defensive to positive approaches or with greater interest in setting up new projects as opposed to expansion investment.

— Trade–related and other disincentive measures in developing countries

The disincentive measures affecting inward direct investment discussed above are clearly much more typical of developing countries in comparison to the OECD countries, as seen from the table in Annex, where almost all developing countries have at least one and normally several such measures. In declining order of importance, the measures most commonly found are local content, local equity, export and transfer of technology requirements.

Approximately two–thirds of the performance requirements considered are of a general nature, applying to all investments. The remaining, sector–specific requirements, tend to be concentrated in sectors such as, in particular, automobiles and related production and, to a lesser degree, in the area of computers, informatics and telecommunications. Sector–specific requirements are most commonly found in Latin America, particularly in Venezuela, Mexico and Brazil. To a very considerable extent, sector–specific measures are in the form of local content requirements. Bearing in mind the difficulties of comparison due to differences in the availability of information as well as the characteristics of the measures themselves, some tentative comparisons with respect to the incidence of measures between broad regions, as well as for individual countries can be made. The region recording the largest number of requirements is Latin America, where particularly Venezuela and Mexico, but also Columbia, Brazil and Ecuador have a substantial number and variety of requirements. For Asia, which records the next highest incidence of measures, countries such as the Philippines, Malaysia, Taiwan and India record several different requirements. Finally, for Africa, where the fewest number of measures are reported, only a few countries such as Egypt, Ghana and Nigeria have more than one or two performance requirements.

Of all the measures examined, approximately one–fifth are linked to incentives or the fulfilment of one particular performance requirement results in the relaxation or non–use of others. In particular, it seems to be local content requirements that are so linked, the only other important category in this respect being local equity requirements, this being so principally for Latin America. When performance requirements are linked to incentives, the main types of incentives are fiscal in nature, including reductions or waivers on import duties, credits or deductions on taxes related to profits, tax holidays and other general tax advantages. In other cases, the "incentive" relates to other performance requirements; for example, local content requirements may be waived or reduced if exports exceed a given level, a given local content requirement has to be met if exports are to benefit from incentives, or local equity requirements may be waived or reduced if a given local content or export requirement is agreed. Where requirements are not linked to incentives, these may relate in one way or another to authorisation or screening procedures; in some instances, authorisation may be conditional on the agreement of requirements, in other cases it has been indicated that it may facilitate or speed up approval procedures.

The measures discussed above are often, but not always, documented in countries' laws and regulations or policy statements. Often, it is not possible to obtain a clear idea of the ways in which these measures are implemented, for example, whether the measures in question are automatic or discretionary, the extent to which they are applied on a case–by–case basis or their degree of negotiability. In addition, the position is often even more vague, where the language describing the policies includes expressions such that performance requirements are in principle, often or may be required, that there may be some pressure to accept them, or that acceptance may facilitate approval or often attract subsidies. These aspects, together with other features of the information available mean that the discussion of these measures must be rather impressionistic and illustrative of regimes in countries or regions. It is important to underline, therefore, that the information available does not necessarily provide for a complete or accurate picture of performance requirements in developing countries.

Measures affecting outward investment

The investment incentive and disincentive measures addressed above concern measures taken by countries in relation to inward investment. This section discusses briefly measures taken in OECD countries as home countries of international direct investment, i.e. concerning outward investment. OECD countries have a generally neutral approach to outward investment. However, and on the incentives side, many have special promotion schemes for international direct investment in developing countries (such as tax credits, soft loans, grants for feasibility studies and guarantees against commercial or political risk).

There are, nevertheless, certain measures in some countries which restrict or act as a disincentive to outward investment, including restrictions on outward investment. Norway and Finland, for example, may restrict outward investment generally while Ireland has restrictions concerning the financing of outward investment, taken for balance–of–payments reasons. Other measures may concern specific sectors such as banking and securities, where Italy and Japan have measures which are related to prudential considerations.

In the course of the Committee's discussion of these measures, the question was raised as to whether measures which affect the exports of foreign located affiliates of domestic companies could have a disincentive effect on outward investment.

c) The treatment of domestic and foreign–controlled enterprises
    in incentives and disincentives policies

In terms of both design and implementation, the general picture in OECD countries is one of neutrality between investments by domestic and foreign–controlled enterprises with respect to investment incentives policies. Thus, with respect to the eligibility or nature of awards, there is generally little discrimination on the basis of nationality in the various incentives measures available to investors. Accordingly, there are very few incentives measures which are either not available to established foreign–controlled enterprises or which are implemented in a manner which would systematically offer lower awards or place more stringent conditions associated with the award of incentives to such enterprises. There are, however, one or two limited examples where this does occur, for example, in Australia, with respect to R&D incentives and in Germany in the tourism sector, but these arise in relation to branches of foreign–controlled enterprises rather than to enterprises under foreign control established in these countries. The typically neutral approach of OECD countries in administering their incentives policies follows from their generally liberal policies to foreign investment and the appreciation of the contribution such investments may make to the domestic economy in areas such as investment and employment levels, transfer of technology, managerial skills and so on.

At the sub–national level, there are some measures where eligibility to a particular scheme may be denied to foreign–controlled enterprises, or are given priority treatment. This is the case in Canada, for example, where not all provincial assistance programmes are accessible to foreign investors.

Just as OECD countries do not generally discriminate against foreign investments in their incentives measures, so too do they not tend to have investment incentives programmes specifically geared to attract foreign investment, although in their efforts to attract foreign investment via overseas missions, fairs, etc., emphasis is also placed, inter alia, on the incentives available to investment. It is equally true, however, that features of incentives schemes in some countries may be especially attractive to foreign investors for example, when special investment packages geared to large projects exist. A major aim of Irish investment incentives policies, for example, has been to attract foreign direct investment and this has met with considerable success in the past. More recently, however, there has been the expression of some concern in Ireland in relation to the need to develop and improve linkages and integration between domestic and foreign–controlled enterprises, particularly between large export–orientated enterprises and local suppliers and Ireland has recently introduced the National Linkage Programme with this aim in mind.

The main types of disincentive measures addressed in this study — host country disincentives (including trade–related investment measures), restrictions on outward investment and other measures are often discriminatory in nature, either by design (i.e. they apply only to foreign investors) or by effect (i.e. they present a greater disincentive effect for foreign investments). Thus, for example, even if local content or local ownership requirements are applied even–handedly to both domestic and foreign investments, foreign investors may be more reluctant or less able to meet such requirements or, at least, they may more often be faced with the need to modify investment projects in a manner which they would not have in the absence of such measures. To the extent that such disincentive measures are found in OECD countries they tend to be exclusively or predominantly operated at the national level.

Section 3.   MAIN FINDINGS AND RECENT EVOLUTION

On the basis of the above description of various features of the investment incentives and disincentives policies in Member countries as they presently exist, this Section attempts to identify important changes or evolutions in these measures which have taken place since the early 1980s. Consideration is given first to the question of whether any general trends can be discerned with respect to the overall use of such measures, i.e. whether Member countries are placing greater or lesser reliance on incentives policies as a whole in order to pursue their industrial, regional and other policy objectives. Following this the discussion turns to assessing possible changing orientations in relation to the objectives and policies to which incentives measures are addressed, beginning with the identification of a number of general themes and then taking in turn each of the main policy areas. For example, can changes in the importance of particular policies such as industrial, sectoral, regional or science and technology policies be discerned, and are there any common trends with respect to the treatment of particular sectors such as services or to groups of enterprises such as small– and medium–sized firms? Finally, developments concerning disincentives measures and conditions associated with the award of investment incentives are addressed.

a)   **Trends in the overall use of investment incentives**

On the basis of the information on which this report is written, a first and very broad conclusion is that there does not appear to be, in aggregate terms, any major trend in the overall level of provision of investment incentives. It is of course difficult to determine this in quantitative terms; it is not possible to quantify all elements of the measures examined, reduce them to a common basis and add them up to determine whether there is a trend in a particular direction. Furthermore, a given policy area is not only a question of expenditure levels but also one of political and administrative organisation, of regulation, of services to industry and of management. Reduced appropriations for direct intervention do not therefore necessarily reflect a reduced commitment to a given policy or a reduced policy effectiveness, but may rather be indicative of attempts to increase the efficiency of policy. Attention must also be paid to the effect of greater degrees of information and transparency in incentives systems which can also cloud assessments of possible trends.

The information provided by Member countries on their incentives systems includes, albeit to varying extents, information on overall levels of expenditure for particular measures or for groups of measures. While this type of information provides certain insights into what has been happening in general over the last years, care must be taken in interpreting such information. For example, in depressed periods, demands for defensive measures may rise, while in periods of expansion, more firms will be investing and availing themselves of incentives. Subject to budgetary ceilings, expenditure on incentives will increase, but this does not necessarily mean that the country concerned has decided to place greater reliance or importance on incentives measures. Equally, reductions in the rate of award for a given measure might be interpreted as a move towards a weaker policy, but again this is not automatically the case.

In fact, what has been happening recently in some countries (for example, in Norway) is that expenditure levels for particular measures have increased significantly in the last few years following the growth of corporate investment. The result in those countries has been that budget allocations were fully utilised, resulting in reduced rates of awards, more restrictive eligibility conditions and/or more selective approval procedures, with more applications being turned down.

Bearing the above in mind, it is nevertheless interesting to review briefly incentive expenditure trends in those countries for which information is available. In Australia, there has been an overall net increase in direct budgetary assistance to industry, although such programmes are of relatively minor importance in comparison to trade–related measures. Expenditure on financial incentives in Austria amounted to (on a net basis) Sch 3.4 billion in 1986, representing a 33 per cent increase over the 1983 level; on a gross basis (i.e., without repayments) the corresponding amounts are Sch 9.5 billion (24 per cent increase). In Germany, the situation as concerns regional policy varies depending on the type of incentive; for example, expenditure on the investment allowance has been lower over 1982–84 in comparison to 1981, expenditure on investment grants has been expanding since 1981/82 while the special depreciation allowance has, in 1984, gone beyond its 1981 level, recovering from a fall in 1982–83. Average annual expenditure levels in Ireland over 1982–84 are much higher than that in the 1970s but, within this, 1984 levels of expenditure in a number of incentives areas (e.g. concerning worker training, small industries and re–equipment) were lower than in 1982, a major exception being incentives for new industries and major expansions. In Japan, and with respect to financial measures, expenditure related to financing and purchase of land for relocation, which is the largest individual area of expenditure, has displayed no particular trend over the 1980–85 period, and this is also the case for expenditure over this period for interest subsidies for the development of industrial areas and for subsidies promoting industrial relocation.

The situation in the Netherlands has also varied, depending on the type of incentive. Expenditure on non–regional financial incentives has generally been falling since 1983, while the costs incurred by the investment premium, which declined immediately after 1979–81, are now considerably higher. The budgetary cost associated with the investment premium regulation (WIR), the most important regional financial incentive, continued to expand until 1984, but fell significantly (from Gld 450 to 300 million) in 1985. Notwithstanding the above, there has in fact been a decline in Dutch regional incentive spending, as the regional component of the WIR scheme is now no longer available (having been abolished in September 1983). Overall expenditure levels by the Norwegian Industrial Fund have grown steadily in the 1981–85 period, particularly in 1985 where expenditure exceeded NKr 790 million. With respect to the components of this expenditure, there have been important increases in industrial loans, loans to R&D and grants, whereas the general trend with respect to loan guarantees has been sharply downward. At a more qualitative level, information for the United States indicates a declining federal involvement in and expenditure on various programmes. In some cases, particular programmes have been terminated and others are now less generous. At the state level, however, measures for economic development are still strong and often expanding despite a general desire to trim budgets.

While the incentive expenditure picture in certain individual Member countries is not without interest, the limited available information does not allow general conclusions to be drawn on expenditure trends. However, what can be said is that there appears to have been neither wholesale withdrawal from nor significant overall increases in the use made of investment incentives in general, although important differences do exist. Nevertheless, there have been important changes or reorientations in investment incentives measures which have resulted from changing underlying philosophies concerning the use made of incentives and reflected, inter alia, in changes in the importance given to particular areas of policy and types of investment incentives measures, as will be seen from the discussion below.

b) **Changing orientations in incentives measures**

In response to major changes in the economic environment and associated changes in the general philosophy underlying the use of investment incentives, the recent period has witnessed important changes in the role of investment incentives. In some cases, such changes represent the adoption of new approaches while in others they reflect the development and expansion of particular trends already apparent in the late seventies.

The information available on individual countries provides many examples of broad policy areas (e.g. industrial, science and technology, regional) which have expanded or declined in importance and of particular investment incentives measures which have been introduced or abolished or which have increased or reduced their coverage and generosity. To the extent that broad trends can be identified and generalised from these changes, which frequently go in different directions in different countries, it does seem that a common approach has been to keep more or less the same armoury of measures but to retarget and redirect them to meet the changes that have been taking place and to increase policy effectiveness.

In this context, this section first outlines common aspects observable in the reorientation of investment incentives measures and then discusses the situation with respect to the main areas of policy (e.g. industrial policy, regional policy, etc.).

General themes

The survey of Member country measures reveals that a major change in the practices of many governments is that of a reduced importance given to the role of incentives. This development can be related to a number of aspects, the most important of which may be linked to the view that incentives may have been distorting certain investment decisions and that a greater emphasis is being given to attract international direct investment by a removal or reduction of restrictions, impediments and other disincentives. Other factors such as budgetary constraints and a certain disappointment with the benefits of particular incentives programmes are also relevant. The reduced importance given to incentives may be illustrated by lower overall expenditure on incentives, generally in respect of particular schemes and/or by the abandonment of specific investment incentives. In the case of the latter, a number of countries (such as Ireland and the United Kingdom) have removed certain fiscal incentives (e.g. in the context of major reforms of their tax, including corporation tax, regimes).

More generally, the major fiscal reforms which a number of Member countries have undertaken or are considering, although falling outside the scope of the measures surveyed, are of relevance for the present study as it is clear that the level and structure of business taxation plays an important role in stimulating investment in general, while differences between countries may influence international direct investment patterns. In line with the broad trends in OECD countries towards greater reliance on market forces to guide investment decisions as well as towards reduced government intervention, there have been important tax reforms in a number of countries aimed at providing broader based incentives to investment through often considerable reductions in corporation tax schedules. This has been the case in countries such as Canada, Ireland and the United Kingdom, while, most recently, the United States is also undertaking a comprehensive reform of its tax system although in respect of the United States, the full implications of the changes being undertaken are not yet clear. For example, and as concerns the provision of incentives at national vis-à-vis sub-national levels, the United States is the clearest, if not the only example in Member countries where investment incentives provided at sub-national levels are evidently predominant, but changes in the federal corporation tax system may have implications for the balance of national vis-à-vis sub-national incentives. One of the main objectives of these changes in Member countries' tax regimes is, in providing broader based incentives to investment through reduced rates of tax, to encourage investment decisions to be based more on business rather than on tax considerations.

A major and general feature of changes in Member countries' practices in the area of investment incentives is that the move from defensive to positive measures, already apparent in the past, has considerably developed and expanded. Policies have moved away from the defensive preservation of outdated industries towards measures geared to stimulate investment in structural adjustment to meet new patterns of supply and demand and to promote the adoption of advanced technolgies. Such "positive" measures are often geared, inter alia, to provide explicit priority to promising, often high risk, innovative ventures, where government efforts seek to promote such investment by stimulating investment demand, improving supply side responsiveness and generally aiming to improve the role played by the market.

There has clearly been a move away from defensive policies that were characterised by reliance on subsidies and selective support measures to minimize negative cyclical effects to policies accepting the discontinuation of activities not likely to be profitable. This has been associated with a scaling down of certain support schemes subsidising day–to–day operations and a recognition that bankruptcy, closure and restructuring are unavoidable facts of economic life. In a number of countries, this is also reflected in lesser emphasis being placed on maintaining employment levels in particular industries and the acceptance of higher rates of adjustment on the labour market in order to pursue higher productivity and increased international competitiveness. There have accordingly been a number of changes in incentives systems, particularly when it has been felt that they have been geared to outdated economic priorities and when they may have distorted investment decisions and choices.

In a number of countries, there has been a shift in emphasis from assistance to maintain enterprises towards measures geared specifically to productivity, the use of advanced technologies and structural adjustment. Changes in the use of existing measures or the introduction of new ones can be illustrated from developments in measures in countries such as Australia, Austria, Germany, Ireland, Japan, the Netherlands, Norway and the United Kingdom to mention but some. Similarly, there have been changes with respect to measures addressing particular sectors; while some countries still maintain sector–specific measures geared to older, traditional industries such as steel, shipbuilding and textiles, a number of countries have reported the introduction of measures geared to the newer, high technology and information–intensive areas. In other countries, and within the general objective of promoting the movement of resources into the new technology sectors, the approach has been less one of shifting sector–specific measures from supporting traditional to stimulating new industries, but rather one where the change in emphasis is reflected in a move from sector–specific schemes to more horizontal measures geared to encourage innovation and the use of advanced machinery and technology industry–wide, as has been the case, for example, in the United Kingdom.

Another theme evident from recent changes in incentives measures concerns changes in the administrative and institutional framework in order to make procedures more simple, straightforward, transparent and "user–friendly". More general steps taken to simplify procedures include those with respect to company registration and start–up as in Denmark and Spain, with respect to taxation and financial markets as in Finland, the administration of regional assistance, as in Austria and the more general burden posed on business by administrative requirements, as in Sweden, where a task force has been set up to simplify regulations on the private sector, in the United Kingdom following a 1985 White Paper entitled "Lifting the Burden" and in Canada and the United States following changes in their corporation tax regimes.

As concerns, more specifically, the administration of incentives schemes, there have been considerable changes, generally in the direction of simplification, acceleration and rationalisation in response to criticisms that incentives schemes were

31

often too complex for many firms, the assistance often came only after considerable delay and the aids were frequently commandeered by the best—informed firms.

Measures to simplify and streamline procedures have also been associated with steps to improve the efficiency of incentives programmes with a general desire to ensure value for public expenditure. This is often reflected in greater attention to, or conditions associated with awards geared to ensuring greater additionality and that investments assisted by incentives display potential for long term viability. For example, in Ireland, there is now greater emphasis in the use of appraisal procedures in awarding grants to ensure commercial viability and that the investment represents good value for state money. Also, major reviews to improve programme efficiency have been undertaken in countries such as Australia, Canada and the United Kingdom which have had the goals of avoiding the undesirable stacking of various forms of assistance, to eliminate overlap and duplication and to improve policy evaluation.

A number of countries have also displayed a clear trend in the direction of decentralisation and deconcentration of measures, the aim being to improve policy delivery by shortening the distance between the aid decision maker and the recipient in order to improve the productivity of the award. Countries such as France, Finland, the Netherlands, Norway and Sweden have considerably devolved decision—making or implementation functions to regional bodies or authorities while Greece has transferred many infrastructure decisions from central government to regional prefectures. As noted in the previous section, moves in this direction cover a spectrum, and while it is evident that quite a number of countries have been decentralising the implementation of incentives policies, in some cases together with decision authority over the smaller projects, neither this, nor other information available, suggests any particular trend with respect to the relative importance of incentives offered at the national vis–à–vis sub—national level.

Incentives relating to industry and innovation policies

Developments in industrial policy, as in other policy areas, tend to be an evolutionary process rather than one characterised by major and abrupt shifts in orientations at any one point in time. Changes in incentives measures (introduction, abandonment, modification) often tend to be country specific, reflecting particular economic, social and institutional conditions of the countries concerned. Within this, however, it is still possible to identify certain fairly broad tendencies.

First of all and as already noted, Member countries continue to move towards and consolidate positive support measures as opposed to the defensive stance often characteristic of the seventies. This is not to say, of course, that measures geared to alleviate the consequences of economic change on particular industries or areas are being abandoned, but such measures tend to be, today, less frequent, less generous and more limited.

Such moves go hand in hand with greater government efforts to improve the general economic climate and encourage greater business confidence as an essential means of stimulating the types of investment required by changing conditions. As such orientations apply to investment incentives, a feature in a number of countries has been the use of general tax reductions, often associated with the abandonment of specific investment incentives or reductions in the rates of award. For example, in France, the system of exceptional depreciation allowances for the purchase of capital goods has been replaced by lower rates of corporation tax on reinvested profits; and in the United Kingdom, the accelerated depreciation allowance, previously the main fiscal incentive, has been phased out and offset by major reductions in corporation tax over the last years. The reasons underlying such changes have varied, but they generally relate to changing priorities for incentives policies, the feeling in countries such as, for example, Finland and the United Kingdom, that certain measures may have been distorting investment decisions. Other reasons include the desire to increase the ability of enterprises to self finance and to improve the mobility of capital towards more productive areas.

The area of incentives measures geared to particular sectors or activities is one where there have been important developments. Looking at this group of measures as a whole, a broad distinction can be made between those schemes geared towards the older, more traditional industries such as steel, shipbuilding, textiles and those directed towards the new generation and typically advanced technology activities such as robotics, aerospace, information technology and biotechnology. In making such a broad division it should be borne in mind that schemes concerning activities in both these areas often have strong similarities. For example, they all promote structural adjustment, either by stimulating investment in new generation industries or by assisting rationalisation and adjustment in traditional activities. Equally, science and technology, R&D and innovation are generally key components of such schemes, either because new generation industries are typically high technology orientated or by promoting adjustment in mature industries via the use of advanced technologies, such as, for example, robotics. This being said, there has been a quite evident expansion of and greater emphasis on sectoral schemes in new generation industries. For the more mature industries the picture is more varied, with certain schemes having come to an end, others extended or adapted and new ones introduced, but the broad picture is one of a general cutback in support for traditional industries.

Looking first of all at measures geared to the more traditional industries, the following examples illustrate what has been happening in different countries. In Canada, the Industrial Renewal Board, established in 1981 to provide a mechanism for industrial adjustment in sectors such as clothing, footwear and textiles, ceased operations in 1986 and, in a similar vein, assistance to shipbuilding has been rationalised. In Austria, sectoral assistance has ended and schemes for paper, clothing and leather and textiles are being brought to a close. In the Netherlands, where all sectoral policy is seen as temporary and supplementary to structural adjustment, aid to shipbuilding has continued and less expensive, temporary programmes for structural improvements have been put into effect in several sectors including textiles and general cargo services. In Germany, aid to promote structural improvement and investment in the steel industry came to an end in 1985.

In a similar vein, in France, for example, measures adopted for the steel industry in 1984 were extended in 1985 with a view to firms in this sector returning to profitability in 1987. In Italy too there is currently a proposal to enlarge the scope of the GEPI (the management agency for state industrial participation) which aims to help redress sectors in difficulty with a view to returning firms to profitability. Japan has introduced a series of financial and fiscal measures to improve the structure of basic materials industries by providing for the disposal of surplus facilities, for business tie-ups and for investment in efficient equipment. As concerns the the value of awards under such schemes, German efforts to reduce federal subsidies are reflected in lower rates of award and reduced expenditure in the Shipyards Programme while aid to the steel industry in Italy expanded, in the form of a higher rate of award for the disinvestment grant.

In respect of trade–related measures particularly geared to specific sectors, Australia, in line with its objective to increase the competitiveness of the automobile industry at lower levels of protection, announced a number of measures in 1984, including a gradual reduction in import restrictions, although the plan for the steel industry, also announced in 1984, provides incentives for increased use of locally produced steel.

Without doubt, there has been a clear cutback in sector–specific schemes aimed at traditional industries. There has also been a move away from industry–specific schemes and towards the general stimulation of particular processes or technologies in industry. This is sometimes associated with their replacement by more horizontal, industry–wide schemes or by reduced generosity in continuing ones. At a broader level, there are also some indications of rationalisation or retargetting of the measures often associated with such schemes, for example the move from specific schemes to ones applying industry–wide as well as towards the general stimulation of particular processes or technologies in industry.

Associated with the latter point has been the expansion of schemes directed to the new generation, high technology sectors and activities. Indeed, a number of common themes appear to be emerging from developments in a wide range of countries. Some of these are quite specific to investment incentives, such as a general increase in funding together with a greater concern with programme efficiency. Here, a number of countries have undertaken reviews associated with, for example, the introduction of new measures to avoid the "stacking" of various forms of assistance and to eliminate overlap and duplication, as in Canada, to devote greater resources to policy evaluation, as in the United Kingdom, or to adapt programmes to improve policy responsiveness to research and technology requirements, as in Australia and Finland. There has also been a tendency to focus assistance on priority areas and while these areas vary between countries, the general emphasis is on new technologies, such as new materials, biotechnology, offshore and marine technology microelectronics, fibre optics, control systems and information and computer technology. Changes in the United Kingdom made in 1982 demonstrate a change of emphasis from sectoral to horizontal support to generally encourage, for example, innovation and the use of advanced machinery as illustrated by schemes such as Investment Support for Microelectronics, the Support for Advanced Manufacturing Project and the Robot Support Programme.

More generally, with respect to R&D there has been increased stress on collaborative research, both nationally and internationally as well as within and between industry and other research organisations. This is being pursued in various ways in different countries. For example, in the United Kingdom more money has been made available for collaborative projects, in the Netherlands and Finland particular programmes have been introduced or extended, while other countries such as Japan and Portugal have established agencies to promote collaboration.

A further trend has seen important developments with respect to the introduction or extension of measures directed to promoting the availability of risk capital via special fiscal incentives such as risk capital credits or tax write–offs to stimulate, in particular, investments in high technology and innovatory projects. Examples of such measures are found in countries such as Australia, Austria, Belgium, Ireland, the Netherlands, Norway and the United Kingdom. Other countries such as Italy have set up rolling funds to assist experimental projects and ventures. Measures of this nature may be general, industry–wide, in other cases they may be reserved, at least to some extent, to priority, advanced technology sectors (e.g. as in Italy) or to R&D (as in Australia and France, for example). There may also be an element of priority being given to small firms to assist their start–up, particularly in innovatory areas as witnessed, for example, by the United Kingdom's Business Expansion Scheme. A different approach to providing capital found in a few countries such as Ireland, the Netherlands and Italy, is that of using public equity participation (generally limited to minority holdings) in new companies. In such cases the state, sometimes via national or regional development authorities, may take out loans to raise the funds required for participations and such participations generally require that the projects concerned are capable of providing sustainable and viable employment.

Considerable emphasis has also been placed on policy delivery, i.e. increasing the knowledge and application of measures and seeking for a more effective transfer of technology. Here, some countries have devoted greater efforts to the provision of advisory services as in the United Kingdom for example, while others, such as Austria and Australia have set up innovation agencies to provide advice and assistance in the fields of innovation and technology transfer. Efforts in other countries to improve technology transfer can be illustrated by the introduction of new legislation, for example the Technology Transfer Act in the United States or using incentives to promote these objectives, as in Ireland where grants are given to assist firms in acquiring new product or process technology.

Regional policy incentives

Recent years have seen important changes in the context and aims of regional policies which in turn have necessitated certain changes to the instruments of regional policy. Not all countries have been moving in similar directions as the nature and severity of the problems they have to deal with and the approaches to these are different. Nevertheless, the aims and tools of regional policy do appear to have been converging to some extent and it must also be borne in mind that, in respect of the various objectives and policy areas to which investment incentives are directed, many Member countries have noted that regional policy continues to be a high priority area.

Looking at the developments in regional policies in Member countries, and simplifying greatly, it may be said that the instruments of regional policy have been evolving in the following directions — there have been overall reductions in direct assistance; policy has become more geographically focused; policy measures have been extended to give greater leverage to new sectors and smaller firms; there has been some move away from automatic and towards discretionary incentives and there have been changes in administrative organisation and procedures.

In many Member countries, direct regional aids and incentives funds have tended to decline since the early eighties following a general increase at the end of the seventies. Obviously such a broad statement needs to be qualified as it is often difficult to distinguish and therefore keep account of the amounts directed to regional development as opposed to other areas while, as mentioned earlier, expenditure on aids is only one of the components of any assessment of the intensity of policy.

35

Nevertheless, there have clearly been budgetary reductions particularly in Denmark and the United Kingdom and also in France. Few countries have increased their expenditure as has been the case in Italy, while in countries such as the Netherlands and Norway, budgetary ceilings have been reached requiring changes in the level of awards or the administration of measures.

The boundaries defining the areas receiving regional assistance have been altered in a number of countries, generally in the direction of greater concentration. In the economic environment which has characterised recent years, it has become more difficult to make clear distinctions between prosperous and depressed areas and countries have been inclined to channel assistance towards the most severely affected areas. In Europe, the proportion of the population covered by assisted regions has fallen considerably since 1980. By the early eighties, only a few countries such as Denmark and the United Kingdom were already engaged in such reductions, but most countries are doing so today.

To the extent that generalisations can be made about the automatic/discretionary nature of award systems, the situation, at least in Europe, had been one where the smaller countries have, by and large, relied on discretionary awards with the larger countries' approach being characterised by an automatic base with discretionary topping up, as for example in France, the Netherlands and the United Kingdom. The weight given to discretionary systems in smaller countries probably reflects the fact that, in having fewer numbers of applications to deal with, discretionary awards may permit greater consistency of approach particularly in relation to the application of conditions associated with the award related to viability, need and incrementality. Recently, and for the larger countries there has been some change in emphasis as the automatic base of some schemes has been cut (e.g., the Regional Development Grant in the United Kingdom and the WIR in the Netherlands) with a switch towards discretionary components of award systems. Such changes have followed expenditure pressures on regional budgets and the growing requirement to prove a need for subsidy on the part of the project. As such, the move towards discretionary awards may be associated with their greater ability to operate at the margin and get better value for money.

Employment generation has always been and continues to be an important goal of regional policy. While the majority of incentives are directed specifically to investment, they have also been linked to employment goals via, for example, employment–specific incentives such as labour subsidies or by employment requirements associated with the granting of awards. In Europe, only a few schemes in a few countries have no job–related award conditions. In the majority of discretionary schemes there are either job–related awards or job creation is considered in the evaluation of projects applying for assistance. A number of countries have cost per job limits on schemes (e.g., Denmark, Germany, Ireland, Sweden and the United Kingdom) while explicit minimum job targets are found in schemes, particularly in Germany, but also in France and Italy. Again, country experiences differ; in many measures with employment conditions associated with incentives, such conditions have often been extended to include job maintenance as well as creation as in Austria and France, for example, whereas in the United Kingdom the ammount of subsidy per job has a ceiling depending on the size of the firm's fixed capital. In other cases, as in Germany for example, special investment grants are available to help

36

create high quality jobs and it is now possible to combine regional and R&D assistance to strengthen structurally weak regions.

A marked tendency in recent years has been a shift towards aid for technological innovation. As noted earlier in the section on industrial and innovation policies, this is not especially a feature of regional policy but rather, one which has been occurring much more generally. Indeed, technology is an element which has been given increasing emphasis throughout the range of microeconomic policies to which incentives are associated.

In the context of regional policy initiatives, the increased emphasis on high technology activities has taken a number of different forms. In Denmark, for example, there have been substantial cuts in regional budgets with the savings explicitly earmarked for general action to promote innovation. Some countries have introduced new measures to promote high technology activity; in Germany, for example, the recruitment of highly skilled personnel and the acquisition of patents or start-up investments now qualify for aid, and in Austria high technologies attract aids for location in industrial restructuring zones. Other countries such as France, Ireland, Norway, Sweden and the United States have taken steps, sometimes via incentives, to improve the dissemination of information about new technologies. In addition, most countries are promoting technology development poles and science parks.

The latter aspect, i.e. the creation of particular zones is, together with other developments in relation to service activities and smaller enterprises, one which, although sometimes linked to regional policy, is also often more general in nature and it is as such that these developments are discussed below.

Export, enterprise and technology zones

In recent years, more countries have introduced or developed particular zones, generally restricted to geographically small areas, to promote exports, stimulate entrepreneurship or assist in the diffusion and use of innovatory technologies. The main "measures" taken with respect to such zones include the provision of particular infrastructures, the use of incentives and/or the simplification or relaxation of particular requirements including taxation and planning controls.

Export processing zones are by no means a new phenomenon and their characteristics are well documented; the zones may be generally used for the storage, processing and assembly of internationally traded goods, merchandise may enter the zone custom-free and may be freely exported. By contrast, enterprise zones are much more a phenomenon of the 1980s. Although longer standing in the United States, such zones are of relatively recent origin in countries such as the United Kingdom and, particularly, France. These zones represent a highly specialised blending of measures for endogenous development and small business and they are often closer to urban rather than regional policy.

The enterprise zone concept arose in recognition of the fact that inner city areas, where such zones are often located, were centres of vital small business but which were being eroded over time, inter alia because of the growing burden of government regulations and restrictions. As such, an important feature of such zones, as in the case in the United Kingdom, is the reduction of government intervention and red tape to promote the working of free-market forces. In the United Kingdom, where 25 such zones have been set up since 1981, the zones attract enhanced capital allowances, enjoy a relaxed planning regime and considerably streamlined administration of remaining controls. While the enterprise zones in the United Kingdom are not part of its regional or inner city policies, those in another major proponent of the concept, the United States, are more closely linked to schemes for urban and social rehabilitation. To qualify as an enterprise zone in the United States, the area concerned has to meet criteria related to the number of unemployed and the level of poverty. Once declared, the zones have substantially reduced local property taxes, concessions on capital gains tax and tax benefits for the use of local labour.

Technology development poles, science parks or the "technopolis" are now found widely throughout the OECD area. Again, this is not a concept new to the 1980s, but it is one which has now proliferated. Generally, a number of such areas have been created in a given country, often in both the more prosperous as well as the depressed areas. In the latter type of area, the idea is often less to create decisive new innovations but more to disseminate innovation and to adapt the activities of sectors and enterprises. The types of measures used in these centres, in addition to direct aid, include services to industry and measures with respect to environmental quality. Again, the geographical or regional orientation of this approach differs between countries. Japan appears to have made it an important factor of its policy for reducing regional disparities, with many of the technopolies sites in outlying areas. Other countries as different as Australia and Belgium focus more on areas of population concentration. "T zones" have been introduced in Belgium, these being government equipped areas to revive activity in depressed urban areas while Australia is conducting a policy of intensifying innovative activity around its capital.

Services

Traditionally, investment incentives were at least designed for, if not also limited to manufacturing activities, but the realisation of the important role played by the service economy has seen an expansion in service sector eligibility for investment incentives. In the areas of industrial and innovation policies, the greater focus of assistance on priority aspects includes the extension of certain measures to service sector activities such as management consultancy and data processing. Equally, in the context of regional policy there have been recent developments in countries such as Austria, France, Germany, Ireland, Norway and the United Kingdom such that regionally exporting or producer service sector activities, especially private services to firms and commerce, are now aided in the same way as manufacturing. For example, regional incentives in Austria have been extended to service activities such as those related to software, while in Ireland the range of activities benefiting from the major incentive — reductions in the rate of corporation tax — has been extended to cover a variety of non–manufacturing activities.

Whereas the earlier approach towards incentives for services activities relied largely on specific service sector schemes, the approach increasingly used today is to expand schemes, initially designed for or restricted to manufacturing, to cover specified service activities, with specific service schemes being downgraded or withdrawn. In countries such as Germany and the United Kingdom for example, previously manufacturing orientated incentives have been extended to cover particular services such as data processing, consultancy and other services related to exports, marketing and innovation. Italy, too, where incentives were very much orientated to manufacturing has now opened up such schemes in similar directions. In fact, the majority of countries now provide support to specified business services.

In general, one or more of the following four components are found in the development of services sector incentives. First, the growth of support for new technology in general helps to stimulate high technology services such as telecommunications and computer services. Secondly, and as concerns employment, general schemes for investment have normally some form of employment component, as noted above, and as such, these schemes can be used to assist services which are employment—orientated. Other service sectors are increasingly capital—orientated and as such benefit from the extension of previously manufacturing—orientated schemes supporting fixed investment. Finally, there have also been some moves towards supporting intangibles such as patenting or licensing, reflecting again links with other developments in incentives policies towards innovation and technology.

Small firms

The eligibility of small enterprises for investment incentives is another feature that has gained prominence in the last years. As noted earlier, the main approach has been better to inform small firms that they are eligible for investment incentives and by improving policy delivery to these firms. In addition, some countries have also introduced new measures specifically orientated to such firms, introduced an element of discrimination in incentives in favour of small firms or redefined others to allow their inclusion via reduced eligibility thresholds or less onerous conditions. Other elements of the "package" of measures aimed at stimulating small business activity include the provision of information, advisory and consultancy facilities and the simplification of administrative procedures. These steps in incentives measures reflect the growing realisation of the important role of small business in terms of, for example, employment generation, innovation and entrepreneurship, and their position in the overall industrial fabric of countries and regions.

The main strands of measures towards smaller enterprises can be summarised as follows. First, a number of countries have taken steps to stimulate the use of new technologies. Secondly, concern with the availability of adequate finance has led to schemes providing loans and loan guarantees in countries such as Canada, Denmark, France, Germany, Italy, Norway, Turkey and the United Kingdom, while in Ireland, advance payments of R&D grants to small firms may be made to encourage their greater use of these grants. Thirdly, steps are being taken to enhance the flow of investment from private as well as institutional sources of capital to small business, as illustrated by measures in Canada, the United Kingdom, Ireland, Germany, Greece and France. For example, in Greece, steps are being undertaken to improve administrative mechanisms and procedures to permit smaller firms to have greater access to government procurement contracts, while the Business Expansion Schemes in Ireland and the United Kingdom are also directed to smaller enterprises. Finally, there has been a significant expansion of schemes to improve the provision of information and advice for small firms, as reflected for example by the creation of information centres in Spain, Local Enterprise Agencies in the United Kingdom and "one stop shops" in Ireland to provide, under one roof, comprehensive information on state aids and services to small firms.

c) Recent developments with respect to disincentives and conditions associated with incentives awards

As is the case with investment incentives, there have also been a number of developments in recent years concerning disincentives and other conditions associated with incentives awards. In some cases, particular trends or developments are quite clear, but in other cases, lack of information on the situation in previous periods means that the discussion of possible developments must be more impressionistic.

On the basis of the information presently available, there has been a clear trend in a number of Member countries towards the removal of *trade-related and other disincentive measures*. In Canada, and associated, inter alia, with changes in the policy regime concerning inward direct investment following the replacement of the Foreign Investment Review Agency by Investment Canada, previous local content and export requirements or conditions have been removed. In Ireland, local assembly requirements associated with car imports, introduced in 1968 to permit the Irish industry to adapt to free trade conditions, came to an end in 1985. In Portugal and Spain, local content and export requirements, tied to the award of investment incentives, have been removed, such that incentives awards now contain no obligations concerning exports or imports. The Portuguese authorities have removed such requirements despite the fact that they feel that certain clauses in technology transfer contracts as well as certain measures taken by home countries of foreign investment provoke trade distortions.

In the case of other measures which may have disincentive effects, for example, local equity requirements, it is more difficult to assess possible tendencies as such measures were not covered in any great detail in the previous work of the Organisation on incentives and disincentives. Nevertheless, it is likely that there has been a move towards the relaxation or removal of such measures in light of general trends in Member countries towards greater liberalisation and the work undertaken in the Organisation with this objective in mind.

In other cases, there has been no change in comparison to the early eighties. For example, sector-specific local content requirements are still operated in Australia while countries such as Denmark, Norway and the United Kingdom still retain policies with respect to bidding procedures in the oil sector which may contain elements of local content requirements. In general, the countries concerned have stated that the objective of their policy is to promote full and fair opportunities for domestic enterprises to compete for contracts.

In the regional policy field, locational control measures have either been abandoned (as is the case for the Selective Investment Regulation in the Netherlands) or relaxed considerably, often to the point where they are seen as posing any major disincentive effect. Such developments can be traced to the fact that unemployment has become in many countries a national concern rather than a specifically regional problem and to the risks inherent in such disincentive measures of restricting (rather than diverting) investment or to the loss of internationally mobile investment projects.

On the basis of the information gathered in the survey, it is clear that there is now a much reduced use of trade-related investment measures in Member countries. In many ways, this is a result to be expected in the light of more general trends in the OECD area towards the liberalisation of their policies concerning foreign direct investment. It may also be that further pressure for relaxation or removal of remaining measures may arise as a result of the inclusion of investment–related measures in the new GATT negotiating round.

Looking finally at the types of *conditions associated with the award of incentives*, there has been a clear tendency towards stricter criteria guiding the application and award of incentives measures. This can be traced to a number of forces including budgetary austerity and the need for greater accountability of the use of public funds, the desire to assist investments which will be viable and accordingly to achieve greater value and real benefits from public expenditure, and the need to promote additionality, i.e. to assist those investments which would not otherwise be realised in the absence of incentives. Various approaches have been used in different countries or in respect of different measures with this purpose in mind. In some cases, the implementation of measures has become less automatic and more discretionary, with a more detailed evaluation of the project applying for assistance; in others, steps have been taken to concentrate or to achieve better targetting of incentives, for example in Australia with respect to assistance to exports or in Austria, Denmark, the Netherlands and the United Kingdom by reducing the areas within which regional incentives apply, to concentrate these on the most seriously affected areas. In other cases, the award of incentives may be conditional on specified self–financing levels to ensure, inter alia, that the investor is willing to back his ideas with his own money (e.g. as in certain measures in Belgium). In Ireland, concern with the value to the economy of investments assisted by incentives (including investments by foreign–controlled enterprises) has led to the introduction of the National Linkage Programme, with a view to developing linkages and achieving higher levels of integration between large, export–orientated firms and small local suppliers. The broad approach has therefore been one of the stricter application of existing criteria (with respect to eligibility, need and viability) rather than the introduction of new criteria or conditions.

Chapter II

EFFECTS ON INTERNATIONAL DIRECT INVESTMENT

The objective of this second part of the report is to examine the effects of international investment incentives and disincentives on foreign direct investment. The Committee has already published in 1983 a report on "Investment Incentives and Disincentives and the International Investment Process"[1]. This Chapter, while recalling the main findings of the 1983 study, focuses on developments since then and also considers a number of topics which were not, or not fully, addressed at that time.

The present analysis of the effects of international investment incentives and disincentives measures taken by host countries for foreign direct investment focuses on those covered in Chapter I of this report. However, as was the case in the 1983 publication, indications are given on a range of measures wider than the scope of the measures surveyed. This concerns two main aspects. First, the effects of developing countries' measures are addressed to the extent that they are comparable in nature, if not in importance, to those of OECD countries, and also, when relevant, in a more specific manner. Secondly, and in order for the picture to be complete, some indications are also given on types of measures which are not covered in the survey referred to above, concerning, for instance, important fiscal measures or trade policy measures. However, for practical reasons there remains a need to restrict the scope of measures addressed. For example, disincentive measures attached to the authorisation of inward investment are not covered although they may have effects similar or stronger than other disincentive measures covered in the analysis, as these measures have recently been surveyed by the CMIT[2] and are analysed in the course of the periodic examinations of Member countries' positions vis-à-vis the Code of Liberalisation of Capital Movements. A number of points need to be underlined to make clear the organisation of the analysis below and/or to indicate some of its limitations. As indicated above, the effects of developing countries' measures are addressed in the report. The analysis in this respect is less well grounded, than is the case for OECD Member countries, where the survey provides for a full and detailed description of the measures concerned. In the case of developing countries, a number of listings of the relevant measures have been produced[3] but these give little indication of whether or how these measures, which often have an important discretionary character, are enforced, or in what respect the policies have changed in recent years, i.e., in a period where the evolution in this respect has been relatively important.

A basic distinction is made herein between incentive and disincentive measures. Even at this broad level, a number of grey zones exist, for example trade protection measures may have disincentive effects on international direct investment to the extent that they restrict the import of essential equipment. The same measures may nevertheless be seen as incentives to invest by foreign–controlled enterprises. However, as a general rule, the grey areas appear quite limited, and are referred to below when relevant.

Methodological difficulties may arise with respect to trade–related investment measures. There are many definitions of what constitutes a trade–related investment measure but it is generally understood that such a measure is expected to have an impact on both investment and trade flows. Trade–related measures thus cover measures which have disincentive effects (such as local content or export requirements) or which may be seen as incentives (such as incentives to production for exports). Accordingly, Section 1 which covers incentives to international investment, also covers the relevant trade–related investment measures, while Section 2 focuses on trade–related investment measures for which the disincentive effects are the most important ones.

As will be seen below, incentives and disincentives frequently operate together, often with clear linkages, e.g., when particular investment incentives are conditional on the fulfillment of certain performance requirements. In fact, it is often the case that one of the main roles of investment incentives is seen as that of offsetting the costs resulting from performance requirements. While some important effects of individual incentive or disincentive measures can be isolated, it is also necessary to examine the impact on direct investment of the overall packages of measures involved, as it is the package with which the foreign investor is faced. Accordingly, while most of the present report addresses individual measures, the latter part of Section 2 discusses the effects of those measures from the perspective of the packages in which they are often situated.

Section 1. INTERNATIONAL INVESTMENT INCENTIVES

The survey of OECD countries' measures in Chapter I has shown that a very considerable array of fiscal, financial and non–financial incentives is available to investors. Although the patterns for developing countries are less well documented, they appear to offer a similar, often wider, range of inducements, albeit in some cases placing greater stress on particular types of measures such as fiscal incentives or free trade zones[4].

This section on the effects of international investment incentives on foreign direct investment is structured into two main parts. The first recalls the principal findings reported in the 1983 OECD publication and, on this basis, the second part examines the implications of developments since that study was completed. In doing so, attention is also given to areas not fully covered in that study such as, for example, incentives at sub–national levels of government and free trade zones.

a) Main results of the 1983 OECD study

Focusing in particular on the OECD area and traditional investment incentives (fiscal, financial, non–financial), the 1983 analysis found, in general, a limited effect of international investment incentives on either the decision to undertake foreign investment (and therefore on its overall volume) as well as the form of such investment (e.g., majority versus minority equity positions, or greenfield investment versus acquisition/merger). Indeed, the main determinants underlying the decision to invest abroad and the form of investment were seen to concern principally market prospects and cost factors in the light of overall corporate strategies.

Investment incentives obviously influence cost considerations, and this may have an impact, particularly during a period characterised by increasing competition for stable rather than growing markets and thus by a heightened cost consciousness. But other cost considerations, seen by business as more permanent or more geared to the fundamental soundness of the project, usually seem to prevail. In other words, and seen from the perspective of the host countries concerned, an investment which would have been specifically attracted by investment incentives may turn out not to be sound in the longer run and require a continuing support that business may not be able to obtain, a situation which is more likely to arise the greater are investment decisions influenced by tax or other incentives vis-à-vis market and commercial considerations.

International investment incentives do not appear to have a significant influence on the timing of investments either. In some cases the timing of such investments may be brought forward, although it may also be retarded in cases where incentives awards are slow in being finalised and paid. Nevertheless, factors such as market and corporate opportunities (as well as negotiations with some governments with respect to their regulations governing inward investment) are likely to be more important determinants of the timing of investments.

Incentives tend to exert a significant influence at a later stage of the decision process, after the basic decisions concerning investment abroad (i.e., the decision to service a particular market or set of markets through establishment rather than through exports) have been taken. However, the general impact of international investment incentives on the broad directions of direct investment flows was also found to be limited, although their effect here is likely to be stronger than that in relation to the volume or modalities of such flows. On the one hand, the decision to serve a particular market (such as North America, Europe or South East Asia) through investment in the relevant world region rather than through export from another region appears to be primarily influenced by market prospects and basic cost considerations. Foreign investors often see the question of location initially in terms of world regions and the choice between world regions (if there is one) is thus determined by factors perceived as having greater significance than the differential provision of investment incentives.

On the other hand, international investment incentives are likely to have a significant impact on the intra-regional location of investment, i.e., the choice of country (and sometimes the location within that country) within the world region relevant to the market the investment is intended to service. If, for example, a multinational enterprise is considering an investment in the European Community to serve that market, differences in the provision of incentives between different countries in the Community may strongly influence the actual country location chosen, along, obviously, with other factors such as the political and economic investment climate, availability of labour of the required characteristics, communications networks, etc.

Of course, the influence of international investment incentives on the locational decisions will depend much on factors such as the overall magnitude of awards or their structure. For example, tax concessions will be less important than some equivalent value grant to investors sensitive to the payback period of the project, the immediate payout associated with grants would in general be preferred, ceteris paribus, to fiscal incentives whose value will depend on the profitability of the investment. In other cases, the visibility and predictability of the incentives measures — and these are features valued by business — may cause some investors to prefer automatic, fiscal incentives over discretionary and project–related grants, although firms may not always be deterred by the lesser transparency of certain incentives measures, where experience and contact with government allow them to reach reliable estimates of the awards that would accrue to them.

An important question on analysing the effect of international investment incentives on intra–regional location decisions concerns the extent to which broad similarities in the incentives systems in competing locations tend to cancel out their influence on this decision. It is often the case that a number of potential country locations within a given world region have relatively similar incentives systems. In these cases the investor may make his choice of location independent of incentives to the extent that he expects a comparable level of assistance irrespective of the location chosen and any survey will show a limited impact of incentives on investment flows, although there may be an impact on trade flows and there would be a clear distortive effect on the allocation of resources. However, this does not mean that any particular country would wish to reduce significantly its investment incentives and therefore that they are without any effect. As a result, significant reduction in incentives seems to require a multilateral approach. Furthermore, there are also many cases where, despite similarities in the incentives systems of countries in a particular region, there are still important differences in the structure of incentive measures and, as indicated in the preceding paragraph, these may be sufficient to avoid the type of stalemate situation suggested above.

Incentives may also influence the choice of location within a given country, particularly when regional policy measures create significant spatial differentials with respect to the value of awards. A number of countries have been quite successful in attracting investment, including foreign investment, to regional problem areas, although the experience has differed considerably between countries[5]. In some cases, incentives have been able to generate new investment in these areas, although in other cases, it appears that the stronger effect has been in relocating or diverting investment from one part of the country to another.

The locational effects of international investment incentives will also differ depending on the country considered. For example, it seems likely that incentives have played an important role with respect to the overall level of foreign direct investment in some countries, Ireland being an example, while in Belgium they have led to a significant impact only on the regional distribution of investment.

There are a number of exceptions to the broad findings summarised above. In some situations, for example, the impact of international investment incentives may not be confined to the intra–regional level. There are some industries, such as microprocessors, which are very footloose in a world–wide context, and others, such as certain parts of the automobile sector for which it is competitive to service the world market as a whole from a single or very few locations. In such cases, incentives are more likely to influence locational decisions from the outset, although their impact on these through their effects on costs must be compared to those of the other cost factors which are often perceived as being more important in the longer term by business. This is the case, for instance, when the investment project contemplated may be followed by as yet unplanned extensions, for which there may be uncertainty as to the availability of incentives. In such a case, incentives concerning the initial investment tend to be compared to other prospective costs concerning the overall long term project.

Other examples exist of where such effects can arise, although these may be more uncertain or limited. For example, international investment incentives may influence the location of investments concerned with the transformation of minerals along the axis between source and market. Cases of competition between countries for such investment via incentives have been documented in the past, although not so more recently due to depressed levels of investment in the mining sector, beyond the extension of existing capacity. A similar possibility concerns the location of major investments in ship repair facilities along traditional cargo routes.

There may also be a few cases where competing locations are, in fact, very similar with respect to the essential requirements or opportunities available to the investment, for example in terms of required infrastructures, labour availability, cost and quality, market prospects and so on. In these cases a particular edge is given to the role played by investment incentives where differences in the magnitude of awards but also differences in their structure may play a decisive role.

Account must also be taken of measures that were referred to but not fully discussed in the 1983 study, such as trade protection measures (tariffs, quantitative restrictions, voluntary export requirements and so on), or the threat of protection. In certain cases, such measures appear to be among the most powerful forces determining the choice of establishment over exports as a means of supplying a given market and, in consequence the location of international direct investment, even at the intercontinental level. Thus, it is clear that some of the general conclusions reached concerning the investment incentives fully surveyed in the 1983 study may not apply when some trade measures are examined from the perspective of their incentive effects on international direct investment.

Nevertheless, and apart from the above comment on trade measures, the types of exceptions discussed in the 1983 report were not seen as significantly altering the broad conclusions found in respect of the influence of international investment incentives on direct investment patterns. On this basis, it is now appropriate to turn to more recent studies and new trends, as well as to investigate areas not assessed in the 1983 study with a view to examining whether earlier findings are now brought into question.

b)   Implications of recent developments

The remainder of this section discusses the results of more recent research and examines the implications of recent trends or developments in a number of areas such as technology, changes in the economic context for international direct investment patterns and developments in investment incentive policies.

Recent research

In comparison to the considerable amount of research into the effects of investment incentives undertaken in the 1970s, there have been relatively few such studies issued during the 1980s, particularly studies taking a more comprehensive approach.

Particularly worth noting is a study by Guisinger and Associates[6] which examined the effects of international investment incentives (and disincentives) on foreign direct investment. The study, published in 1985, and covering therefore roughly the same period as the OECD 1983 study, examined 74 investment projects in both developed and developing countries and focused on four industries, each likely to react differently to incentives and performance requirements — automobiles, computers, food products and petrochemicals. The conclusions of the study, that incentives of one sort or another were often an important factor in the location decision in the majority of the projects examined, point to a role of incentives which appears to be significantly wider than seems to emerge from the OECD 1983 study as well that in other research. There are, nevertheless, a number of differences between the Guisinger and other studies which seem to explain this apparent discrepancy.

First of all, the Guisinger study uses a much broader definition of incentives which, in addition to fiscal, financial and non–financial investment incentives also includes commodity protection measures and also what he calls "implicit" measures (such as the anticipated availability of government purchasing contracts). As has been noted above, trade protection measures can exert a very powerful influence on international direct investment and, indeed, Guisinger found that trade protection was in many cases a key factor in influencing investments, in particular, for a protected domestic or common market, with a lesser effect on investments geared to world markets. Other investment incentives, by comparison, appear to have little influence on decisions concerning investment in protected markets, but may play a stronger role for investments geared to serve a regional or world market. This is in line with the results of the OECD 1983 study.

A second and more general point concerns the way in which the effects of incentives are identified[7]. Guisinger, as do other researchers, used the approach of defining a counterfactual situation whereby the effect of incentives is indicated by the difference between what actually happened and what would have happened in some other, hypothetical situation. In the Guisinger study, this took the form of examining whether there would be changes to investment decisions concerning a given country on the assumption that that country removed *entirely* all of its measures while others kept theirs. In contrast, the 1983 OECD study reported on research where the effects of incentives were evaluated especially or implicitly from the more usual point of comparison involving only realistic, limited *changes* in the policies. Thus, it is not surprising that such research points to lower effects than approaches such as that in the Guisinger study. As Wells[8] points out, once account is taken of methodological, coverage and definitional questions, the results of the Guisinger study are not inconsistent with, indeed they confirm, the results of other studies which used a more limited definition of incentives.

An interesting finding in the Guisinger study, and a topic generally not treated in other studies, concerns what he calls "implicit" incentives. While most incentives are explicit, i.e., framed in national laws and regulations, implicit measures operate through the discretionary powers which governments possess concerning the treatment of enterprises after the investment is made. Examples include the expectation or promise of government purchases or the removal or relaxation of certain conditions on the operations of the enterprise if a certain investment is made. Such implicit incentives were found to play an important role in a number of the projects examined by the Guisinger study, a finding which suggests that current definitions of investment incentives may not be sufficiently encompassing.

Obviously, the effects of international investment incentives on foreign direct investment will depend on a variety of factors such as the countries involved, the purpose of the investment, sector etc. Studies focusing on the *developing countries* generally reach conclusions similar to those discussed earlier for the OECD area[9]. For example, studies by Root and Ahmed[10] and Hagaki[11] found no statistically significant role and a Group of Thirty study[12] concluded that tax advantages and other inducements were regarded as relatively unimportant influences on the investment decision; even while they may tip the balance in favour of a particular location in certain circumstances, this possibility was found to be rare. In many cases, it seems that the main role played by incentives is in offsetting the "tax" resulting from performance requirements. Indeed, Lim[13] found a negative relationship between international direct investment and investment incentives, supporting the view that incentives are often seen with respect to their ability to offset costs resulting from performance requirements which themselves are generally perceived by business as disincentives. A study by Nankani[14] did find a prominent role for government policy, but here the emphasis was on general attitudes to international direct investment rather than specific investment incentives.

Particularly when looking at the effects of international investment incentives in developing countries, a number of the studies referred to above indicate that it is important to consider the basic purpose of the investment, i.e., whether it is for *import substitution or geared to production for export markets*[15]. For investments intended to produce for the local market, investment incentives are unlikely to have an important influence[16]. It is the existence of a specific and often protected market which motivates the investment and determines location, and for the investor, the decision is generally whether or not to service a particular market, the presumption being that it would have to be serviced from a location in the country concerned. A more influential role for incentives may exist for export–orientated investment. Not only may there be a real choice of location between competing countries, but such investments, which will have to be competitive internationally, are also more closely based on cost considerations[17]. However, it is not always possible to make clear distinctions between local market and export investment as both purposes may be served by the same unit. Recent developments may have reinforced this trend. Developing countries traditionally pursuing import substitution strategies may now be devoting more attention to exports than previously for reasons related to debt financing difficulties, while as income levels rise in traditional export–platform countries, this will develop local demand for various goods and services.

Sectoral characteristics are also important. For example, in highly footloose industries, such as certain parts of the computer industry, incentives may significantly influence location decisions, for instance by making an attractive location more attractive[18]. This may also happen in certain parts of the automobile industry. However, for other parts of that industry, the very high start up costs of investment make long–run profitability a crucial concern and, in protected developing country markets, trade incentives are the dominant influence. The Guisinger study reports that for the automobile projects surveyed the investment would anyway have gone ahead in the absense of incentives (and requirements), as market access was the crucial factor[19]. A similar conclusion was reached in his investigation of investments in the food processing sector, where one–third of the firms surveyed indicated that the investment would not have been made in the absense of protection. In this, and other resource–based investments, locational choice takes a fragmented approach, with firms investigating individual locations with respect to the cost, availability and quality of resources rather than one of global or regional scanning. As such, incentives other than trade measures have not been found to be an important determinant.

The results of the studies reported above are broadly in line with the findings of the OECD 1983 study. Even these studies, however, have not investigated the most recent developments in foreign direct investment patterns and international investment incentives measures and it is to the possible implications of these that the discussion now turns.

Changes in the economic context for international investment

It does not appear that investment incentives have played any major, new role in respect of the two basic changes in the economic context for international investment over the last years — the substantial increase of international direct investment in the United States and the falling share of the developing countries in general and Latin America in particular[20]. Rather, these changes confirm the importance of growth and market prospects. In addition, and as concerns the United States situation, two further points may be noted. First, market access issues and the perception of risks for market access in the United States are likely to have played a significant role in the recent expansion of international direct investment in the United States, notably Japanese investment. Secondly, as noted by Hufbauer and Clapp[21] individual states have been using incentives to international investment more frequently, often through the same types of measures, including the tailor–made package approach. It now seems that two previously separate spheres — competition between countries and competition between areas within a country — for international direct investment may now be beginning to merge as sub–national units compete directly with other countries to attract international direct investment. In relation to developing countries, and in addition to the role played by growth and market factors, it is also likely that perception by business of the investment climate has seriously deteriorated — despite some of the policy changes concerning the regimes applicable to inward direct investment, discussed in Section 2 below — and essentially as a result of the debt situation of those countries and the ensuing difficulties for conducting business which may result, for instance, from controls on imports, limits set to the repatriation of profits, etc.

As pointed out earlier in this section, and already noted in the OECD 1983 study, the nature of *technological change* (in electronics, computer and telecommunications services, etc.) may be such that the role of international investment incentives is enhanced in some sectors. The scope of activities which are footloose in a worldwide context, or for which it is competitive to service the world market from one or a very small number of locations, is likely to have increased[22]. Countries that were not previously competing with each other for international direct investment (e.g., such as Ireland and Singapore) may now be doing so and, in part, on the basis of incentives packages. *Corporate strategies* have been adapting to the wider dimension given to locational choice by technological change. Other developments in corporate strategies, however, go against the idea of an enhanced influence for incentives. For example, when the strategy involves the concentration of activities on fewer bases which are highly integrated with each other, it would seem that more attention is paid to the context of fundamental and longer term requirements, in which investment incentives are generally not perceived by business to belong.

Changes in policies

An important trend evident from the survey of Member countries' investment incentives policies has been a certain withdrawal from and associated reduced expenditure on awards to industry. Up until the early 1980s there had been a continuous expansion in the use of government aid, which increased from 1.15 per cent to 1.87 per cent of GDP in the OECD area over the period 1970 to 1983. Since then, almost all Member countries have begun to retreat on a number of fronts, particularly with respect to subsidies to specific industries or enterprises. At present, however, there is little statistical evidence available to show the extent of disengagement. A related trend has been the reorientation of incentives measures, particularly from defensive support for declining industries towards greater concentration on growth and technology areas as well as towards vertical (rather than sector–specific) schemes.

According to a recent OECD study on "Structural Adjustment and Economic Performance"[23] that review of the role of assistance has not always arisen from an in–depth reassessment of the overall social and economic costs and benefits of that aid. Developments can in fact be traced to various forces. At the broadest level, the declining reliance placed on assistance may be linked to the broader process underway in the OECD area towards reduced government intervention, while general pressures to reduce budgetary costs associated with assistance have also been influential. Other forces more directly related to the incentives schemes themselves include a certain disappointment with the benefits that have resulted from a number of programmes, where in some cases it is felt that incentives have not resulted in sufficient additionality and that incentives may have been distorting certain investment decisions. There may also be a growing feeling that certain types of investment incentive measures, particularly those of a sector–specific nature, are more difficult to design and implement in a world where industrial problems are increasingly transsectoral and transnational and where demarcation between individual sectors or products is becoming blurred by technological developments.

The same factors seem to have led to efforts to make remaining incentives more efficient. As indicated in the survey of Member countries policies, these efforts are often reflected in increased attention to, or conditions associated with, awards geared to ensuing greater additionality and that assisted investments display potential for long–term viability. In some countries, these moves have been associated with major reviews of investment incentives programmes to eliminate overlap or duplication and to improve programme efficiency. However it seems likely that in the general context of reduced budgets for investment incentives and reduced levels of awards in individual

51

schemes, and despite the greater efficiency that may be achieved from the types of developments just referred to, a significant increase in the effect of investment incentives cannot be expected.

An area not fully covered in the OECD 1983 study, and where important changes have occurred which may have noticeable effects on international direct investment, concerns corporate tax policy. Major fiscal reforms have taken place since 1983 in Canada, the United Kingdom and the United States and are presently being considered by other countries such as France, Germany and Japan.

As noted in a recent OECD publication[24], advocates of the types of changes referred to above have argued that business does not place fiscal measures among the major investment determinants and thus the provision of tax incentives may only result in cost and price distortions rather than in any effect on the magnitude of investment, as intended. It is also felt that while a strong case can be made for specific, well-targetted assistance to promote new products or technologies, fiscal concessions are a blunt instrument, difficult to target or focus. As such, the approach taken in the reforms of fiscal systems has been to simplify their structure, reduce tax rates and broaden tax bases as well as to abolish specific fiscal incentives and provide a greater role to the market.

Assessments of the possible influence of changes in fiscal policy on overseas investment have often led to conflicting results. Frisch and Hartman[25], for example, found that foreign tax rates may be of importance; Vernon[26], however, argued that the investor weighs a few percentage points difference in overall tax rates as an economic factor of only trivial significance, while Fullington[27] shows that there are very large differences in effective tax rates by sector and by type of activity.

The types of fiscal changes outlined above are too recent to provide hard evidence on their effects on international direct investment. A fuller assessment of their impact must take account of a variety of factors such as what will be done with unused tax credits and whether other countries will react to counter what they may percieve to be a resulting incentive to inward investment in countries which have lowered effective tax rates. What does seem clear, however, is that multinational enterprises will have to pay greater attention to international differences in tax rates when considering international direct investment decisions.

It is not yet clear how international direct investment patterns will be affected, but there will likely be some rethinking of where to set up new operations and a review of existing ones (particularly if there is excess capacity at home). Significant foreign disinvestment is not expected when home country tax levels, as a result of tax cuts, are significantly below those in host countries, but there may be a reduced attraction to open up new subsidiaries in the latter as credits for tax paid abroad will now cover a smaller proportion of the home country tax bill which may therefore increase the cost of doing business abroad. For multinational enterprises based in relatively low tax countries, there may also be a tendency to shift profit back to the home country (with possible implications for the foreign subsidiary). In any case, effective tax rates in different countries may play a greater role in international direct investment decisions in the years to come.

Free trade zones

Another policy development which, although not new, has gained greater importance in recent years is that of free trade zones through which important packages of incentives are increasingly offered. For example, the number of free trade zones in the United States expanded from seven to over 150 in the period 1970 to 1984. In the developing countries, export processing zones increased from 79 in 25 countries in 1975 to 176 in 46 countries in 1986. There are of course important differences between different types of zones and countries with respect to their ability and even intention of attracting international direct investment.

Certainly, export processing zones (EPZs) in developing countries have generally been set up with the specific aim of acting as a focal point for international direct investment. In some cases, it may be the only way to enter a country as a result of government policy; in others it may certainly facilitate entry by providing investment incentives and basic infrastructure not always available throughout the country, while certain requirements or restrictions may be removed or relaxed within the zones[28]. Although they provide attractive sites and conditions for international direct investment, EPZs have not proved a universal success story, as suggested by Kreye, Heinrichs and Fröbel[29], as site selection has to fit with corporate strategies on rationalisation, technology and structure. In some countries, therefore, EPZs may be a necessary but by no means a sufficient requirement to attract international direct investment. Nevertheless, and as shown in a study on the experience of Asia by Maex[30], EPZs in this region acted as a strong focal point for international direct investment, a considerable part of which was directed to the burgeoning zones and which was associated, in turn, with the strong export performance of many of the countries of the region[31].

In the OECD area, free port zones (FPZs) were often inspired by the objective of attracting investments in low volume/high value manufacturing goods such as electrical goods and electronic components. The attractions offered by FPZs include improved cash flow (by exemption from customs duty, postponement of VAT until goods are released on the domestic market), greater flexibility (for example, by permitting duty–free storage of goods until market prospects improve), the relaxation of administrative controls and other benefits resulting from the concentration of certain facilities within the zone[32].

The benefits expected from FTZs in the OECD area have sometimes been questioned, it being felt, for example, that their performance in attracting investment has been lacklustre, with a stronger role being that of diverting investment into the zones from other parts of the country. A study by Balasubranumyam and Rothschild[33] found that FPZs in the United Kingdom were in direct competition with their counterparts in developing countries (where incentives and related measures are often much more attractive) while their attractions with respect to cash flow and flexibility, as defined above, were of little relevance to investors from the EC. For investors from other areas they were found to offer few tangible benefits outside customs duty exemption, although they may be an attractive means of getting around import quotas by some reprocessing of goods to be sold on the domestic or common market and paying of the relevant duties. In other cases, such as the United States, an important function of free zones seems to be as entrepôts, where the main activities often tend to be labelling and distribution of goods for the local market rather than the transformation or production of goods for export markets.

Notwithstanding the qualifications made above, FTZs do represent one of the few policy areas related to incentives where there appears to be growing international competition for direct investment. While their performance up until now may not have fully lived up to expectations, the growth in the use of FTZs suggests this to be an area of increasing interest, particularly in the developing countries and in the light of developments in multinational enterprises strategies, trade frictions and technology changes. The growth of and competition between EPZs has certain parallels with what has been recently happening in the case of financial centres, although here, competition has so far not generally been related to incentives aspects, but rather to the liberalisation of restrictive measures.

*
*   *

All in all, the above discussion of recent studies and developments concerning international investment incentives and foreign direct investment tends to confirm the broad conclusions of the OECD 1983 study. In particular, it is striking that while recent competition for international investment has been increasing in the financial and other sectors, as a result of present economic circumstances, investment incentive schemes do not seem to have been involved in any major way. Rather, and because of the effects of, inter alia, budgetary constraints, the most important feature of the competition has been the increasing emphasis, in OECD countries and to some extent in certain developing countries, on attracting international direct investment by a removal or reduction of restrictions, impediments or other disincentive measures in line with a broad and pronounced trend, especially in the OECD area, but also in a growing number of non–Member countries, towards the liberalisation of policy regimes concerning inward direct investment and its subsequent treatment after establishment. Of course, the above does not imply that competition for investment through incentives has been totally eradicated. Many countries would not wish to eliminate their investment incentives as this would seem to them to reduce their chances to attract investment. In fact, important reductions in investment incentives would seem to require a multilateral approach.

Changes in the economic context for foreign direct investment and developments in international investment incentives policies, as well as more detailed analysis of a number of elements not fully addressed in the 1983 study also have to be taken into account. Of particular importance are the development of footloose industries at the world level, the impact of trade protection measures, the development of free trade zones and, although their impact is as yet still unclear, major changes in tax policies. These features may tend to widen the qualifications made to the results of the 1983 study.

Section 2.   DISINCENTIVES AND TRADE–RELATED INVESTMENT MEASURES

This section discusses host country measures which have a disincentive effect on direct investment flows from abroad.   The types of measures addressed include a variety of measures such as local content requirements (whereby some percentage or absolute amount of inputs is to be produced locally or purchased from local sources), export requirements (whereby some level — percentage, absolute amount — of production is to be exported), trade–balancing requirements (whereby exports should ammount to some proportion of imports), product mandating requirements (whereby the investor should export certain products exclusively from the host country to regional or world markets),   technology transfer requirements (which require that specified technologies should be transferred, that they are transferred on arbitrary terms and/or that specific levels of R&D be conducted), local equity requirements (whereby a certain ceiling — sometimes progressive — is set on foreign equity), licensing requirements (which concern the production, use or sale of products or technology in the host country and often define the level of royalties to be received by the investor), exchange and remittance restrictions (which may limit the repatriation of profits or capital related to the investment, limit access to capital, etc.), manufacturing requirements or limitations (which may require the production of particular goods or lines or which may restrict the ability to produce particular goods or operate in particular sectors i.e., market reserve), and various other restrictions and requirements concerning, for example, financing, the modality of the investment (e.g., concerning mergers and acquisitions or concerning branches and subsidiaries) or investment into unrelated areas.

Obviously, many of these measures can be seen as trade–related investment measures, as they do also appear to have an impact on trade flows, this being especially the case for the first ones listed in the above paragraph, where their impact on trade flows appears to be intentional and quite direct.   However, and as indicated earlier, trade–related investment incentives are not discussed in the present section which focuses on the disincentive effects of measures.

It should also be borne in mind that the present section does not fully cover restrictive measures related to the authorisation of investment.   Indeed, these measures, when they concern investment by non–residents, have been surveyed separately in a recent OECD study entitled "Controls and Impediments Affecting Inward Direct Investment"[34] and they are regularly addressed in the periodic OECD examinations of Member countries' positions under the OECD Code of Liberalisation of Capital Movements[35].

The present section starts by recalling a number of general points as to the nature of the effects of the measures concerned on international investment flows, that were already underlined in the 1983 OECD study.   It then gives a number of more detailed indications on the investment effects of such measures considered independently from incentives measures with which they are nevertheless often associated.   The present section is concluded by discussion of the effects of these measures where, on the contrary, they are viewed as part of a package.

a)   General effects

As already noted in the OECD 1983 study, the effects of disincentives measures such as those referred to above on investment flows may be wider than those of international investment incentives, as is clearly and obviously the case when investment in certain areas or activities is simply prohibited, or when conditions or requirements to be fulfilled in order for the investment to go ahead are so onerous that they are unacceptable to a wide range of enterprises regardless of other attractions or incentives.   Even if the investment is permitted subject to preconditions or performance requirements, or when these conditions are attached to the award of incentives, such measures are generally perceived by business as indicative of the overall business climate in the country concerned and of its policy approach towards international direct investment, and this is even more so in the present period of heightened risk and uncertainty: in other words the influence of the measures concerned on investment decisions may be considerably broader than the actual costs they would impose on investment projects.

Disincentive measures can obviously influence the location of international direct investment, and this influence may extend beyond locational choice within a given world region when, for example, the nature of preconditions or performance requirements in a country (or in the countries of a given world region) cause the investment not to go ahead at all or to be realised in a different world region[36]. More generally, however, it is likely that the locational impact of such measures is on the choice of a location within a region, with investment moving to the country or countries in that region with less restrictive disincentives regimes. Disincentives may also affect other aspects of international direct investment decisions, for example, when local equity requirements interfere with the intention of some enterprises for full or majority ownership or when joint ventures are required by the host country.

In other cases, the effects of disincentives may be more subtle, but nevertheless real.   For example, local equity requirements may in some cases not prevent the investment from going ahead, but may result in changes to the structure of the unit or the nature of the activities conducted internal to the locally established enterprise and may affect its links with other parts of the organisation.   For example, local equity requirements may cause parent involvement in foreign affiliates which have a high technological content to increase in decision areas such as that concerning product introduction, as a result of greater concern to safeguard patents or to maintain quality control.   Similarly, companies with a considerable degree of integration between affiliates in different countries may be less likely to transfer decision–making authority, in areas such as the decision to enter new markets, as domestic ownership and say could affect interdependences and relations between affiliates in different countries[37]. In other situations, measures relating to the possibility of disinvestment, for example concerning repatriation of profit and capital, may lead a firm to forego investment in the first place. Another effect reported as frequently arising, is that measures such as local content or export requirements may result in larger, but less sound investments.

While some host countries may not contest the significance of the types of disincentive effects discussed in the above two paragraphs, they may argue that they use preconditions and performance requirements in order to gain or ensure specific benefits from international direct investment which would not otherwise accrue as a result of market imperfections and what they consider to be non–competitive practices of multinational enterprises. A full assessment of this matter is, however, outside the scope of the present report; not only is there a very considerable debate on this subject, but it would require a detailed assessment of market imperfections, multinational enterprise practices and appropriate policy responses.

Nevertheless, the essential point to be emphasised is that beyond their economic impact per se or the market correction argument, preconditions and performance requirements are seen by investors as disincentives and as indicative of the investment climate in the host country, including the treatment of private investment in general and international direct investment in particular. This basic perception does not appear to be attenuated much by the fact that the countries using preconditions and performance requirements also often offer investment incentives, which are frequently seen by business as necessary to offset the additional costs resulting from performance requirements[38]. It is also, of course, preferable from the point of view of business when conditions and requirements are associated with the award of investment incentives as business will be in a freer position to decide whether or not to accept the conditions (and incentives) and proceed with the investment, in comparison to situations where they are linked to authorisation or when requirements are placed on further investment by existing foreign–controlled enterprises. In the latter case, the initial investment may be to some extent captive or locked in, such that requirements, which might not be accepted by initial investors may have to be accepted. Overall, however, the opinion of business in general is quite clear — they would normally prefer a situation of no incentives and disincentives to one where both exist.

b) Effects of individual measures

While a considerable number of studies on disincentives, particularly trade–related investment measures exist, many of these deal largely with the incidence of trade–related investment measures (by country, sector, etc.) or their effects on trade flows[39] with relatively few[40] examining in detail their investment effects.

Outside those cases where performance requirements are self–defeating, i.e., their nature or level is such that they discourage the investment (and the expected gains the host country aimed to achieve from their use are therefore lost), an effect often resulting from trade–related investment measures such as local content or export requirements, as noted above, is a larger but less sound investment than might otherwise have occurred. In the case of export requirements, a larger investment may arise following the higher scale of production required to meet markets the investment had not intended to serve. Local content requirements may obviously result in changed trading patterns, but depending on the nature of the requirement, (i.e., if set in terms of local production rather than purchases from domestic firms) the company may decide to produce locally, itself, certain inputs, which it might otherwise have imported, in order to ensure quality, delivery, etc. More generally, new, higher or additional requirements imposed retrospectively may require further investment, via a type of ratchet effect, to meet new requirements. It may also be that a higher than intended investment may be proposed by the enterprise as a bargaining counter against lower or removed requirements. In addition to the above possible effects on the size of the investment in the host country concerned, there may also be implications for investment in the home or third countries, particularly for example, when they are associated with changed trading patterns which may in turn cause some displacement of investment elsewhere in the enterprise as a whole.

While measures such as local sourcing or export requirements may appear in many cases not to be a major discouragement to investment (due to other factors such as the attractiveness of the location and, particularly, protected markets and/or because their additional costs may be offset by investment incentives), a stronger effect in these respects is often felt to exist in the case of measures concerning technology transfer and local equity participation. For example, where proprietary technology is a key element of the firm's competitive advantage, it may be most reluctant to transfer technology, particularly if it is felt that there is inadequate protection of intellectual property rights or if the technology mandated is not justified by economies of scale, market prospects or competitive conditions[41]. In cases where the requirement is accepted, changes in product levels, mix and pricing may be required to gain an economic return on the investment in technology which may have longer term implications for the overall viability of the investment.

For some firms, depending on aspects of their business philosophy, the retention of authority may be very important. As such, they may be reluctant, if not totally opposed to its diminution, which would result from local equity requirements. While other firms may be prepared to accept such conditions (which often take a progressive nature), particularly if increasing local participation is associated with reduced risks and cost to the firm, it is not always the case that the latter do result, particularly when managerial expertise is weakened. The importance of the latter is indicated in a study by the Conference Board[42] which found that it was not so much the existence of requirements on local equity or local management per se which were decisive factors, but rather more traditional factors such as the quality of the management as well as the size of the unit and the length of establishment in the host country. Nevertheless, the severity of requirements, if not discouraging the investment, may, as noted above, cause the company to limit the structure of the foreign unit such that it still meets host country demands, but with other activities or functions provided by the parent as necessary. Finally, as concerns local equity requirements, a feature particularly typical of this requirement (although often found in others) is that of linkage with other requirements. For example, the acceptance or achievement of, for instance, some local content or export performance may result in no, or a lower level, local equity requirement. As such, this type of measure may be indirectly or implicitly associated with the types of effects discussed above for other measures.

Other types of disincentive measures restricting or limiting the scope of an enterprise's investment or activities may have an impact extending beyond the particular investment project, with implications for the enterprise as a whole in areas such as overall profitability or corporate strategy. For example, restrictions on one aspect of business may not only restrict the enterprise from competing on an equal footing with domestic enterprises, but also any resultant reduction in market share may hinder the realisation of economies of scale or may not justify particular R&D expenditures. Restrictions concerning acquisition or merger with domestic firms may close–off what is for some enterprises a currently important strategic approach to international involvement, while the discriminatory use of government procurement policies may preclude access to lucrative markets and have long–lasting effects on the economic health of the enterprise.

Other aspects of disincentives measures are also quite relevant to their impact on investment flows. Preconditions or performance requirements may be applied in an automatic, mandatory manner or there may be considerable flexibility and discretion as to when they are applied, at what levels, or their trade–off with other requirements[43]. Automatic requirements present a take–it–or–leave–it situation, but they may also be more transparent and predictable, permitting the investor to take better account of their implications and make more optimal decisions. Other investors may feel that discretionary requirements leave room for manoeuvre and may permit negotiation to some level acceptable to both parties. Contacts with government or previous experience may also allow the investor to reach fairly reliable estimates of the impact on the investment. In some cases, the requirement may even be in the form of a best–efforts approach by the enterprise in specific areas. More generally, the extent of effective policing and penalty schemes will influence adherence or compliance with requirements.

It is also important to distinguish between situations when requirements are set out before the investment takes place as opposed to imposition (or stricter application) retrospectively. In the former case, business is in a better position to decide whether or not to accept the requirement and proceed with the investment, whereas the latter case may compel compliance, either to protect an existing investment or market situation, or because of the costs or indeed feasibility associated with alternatives such as disinvestment. These points complement those noted below in the discussion on individual sectors, concerning problems with the security of agreements reached.

The level at which requirements are set is also clearly relevant. As noted earlier, if they are set at unacceptable levels, they will be self–defeating. In other cases, the level at which they are set may in a sense codify what the firm would anyway (or eventually) have done, causing therefore, no effective alteration to the investment except, perhaps, the timing and phasing of certain elements. Nevertheless, should the situation of the firm alter, such "redundant" requirements may become effective ones unless their level can be renegotiated.

Sectoral features

The types of effects considered above may be expected to vary, inter alia, by sector of activity, as indicated, for example, in the Guisinger study. The four cases found in that study, where performance requirements were instrumental in determining the location of the investment, all concerned the *automobile* sector. Those enterprises either already had investments in the country concerned and new, defensive investment was required to preserve access to the domestic market or they accepted performance requirements to maintain market shares previously gained by exports. In respect of the various types of requirements, foreign currency or trade balancing was found to be less of a problem than local content and insistence on local partners (because of problems such as the quality and price of local supplies), price controls and repatriation restrictions. A particular problem for this sector was that of the security of the agreement reached as a result of frequent changes in requirements, which were felt to affect the continued operation of activity and longer–term profitability.

In the *food processing* sector, the lack of national treatment, restrictions on repatriations and the payment of technical fees, price controls and employment requirements were found to weigh heavily on the investment decision as they influence the competitiveness and profitability of the investment as well as external relations with the parent company. Local content and export requirements were frequently used together and while the former was found to have little real impact (as the firm will anyway use local foodstuff inputs), export requirements were seen as particularly burdensome and sufficient to cause particular investments to be abandoned.

In the *computer* industry, where proprietary technology is jealously guarded, the firms investigated in the Guisinger study tended to be very reluctant to accept requirements related to ownership and technology transfer. Some of these firms decided not to invest because of the existence of performance requirements; in other cases, performance requirements were found to have substantially altered export and import plans while a rather frequent impact appears to be in bringing forward certain developments (e.g., with respect to export volume, use of local inputs, etc.) which the enterprise would anyway have done, but at a slower pace. Reluctance to accept ownership and technology requirements in this sector appears to be particularly characteristic of United States investors, who have a primary role in that industry, whereas Japanese investors appear to be less reluctant to agree to performance requirements, in part as they may have a weaker bargaining position and in part in order to ensure market entry. However, as Japanese investment in this area increases, this may result in some change in the strategies of United States firms in respect of performance requirements, in which case the influence of these measures may change in the future.

c) Effects of the package of incentives and disincentives

Of course, disincentives and trade–related investment measures often exist in combination with incentives in many countries, particularly developing countries[44]. In fact, and taking a wider view of incentives, the situation in some developing countries is one where trade protection, performance requirements and investment incentives are frequently found together. This raises the question of why such countries operate a package of measures containing incentives and disincentives rather than having neither of these types of measures, particularly when a main function of incentives, at least as seen by business and particularly in relation to the developing countries, is to offset the additional costs resulting from performance requirements.

Some insight into this question can be gained by examining the rationale behind the use of various types of measures and their implications for international direct investment. In those developing countries which have pursued an import–substitution strategy, the use of various trade measures to protect the domestic market represents a major incentive to foreign investors to establish and produce in that market vis–à–vis supplying it by exports. As discussed earlier, market prospects is one of the primary determinants of the location of international direct investment and in such countries it is trade protection which effectively makes the market. Indeed, the strength of the attraction of protected markets may be such that some countries feel this permits or at least facilitates the use of preconditions and performance requirements in order to ensure or gain additional benefits from the resulting investment.

However, it is not only protected market developing countries which operate disincentives and requirements and as such it is necessary to take a broader look at the rationales for such measures. In some countries, developed and developing, the objective underlying the use of conditions and requirements is to ensure proper accountability and value for expenditure on investment incentives. This situation applies most specifically, therefore, when the measures are attached as conditions to incentives awards. In other situations, preconditions and performance requirements are used to help achieve national economic objectives in a variety of areas such as investment, employment, balance of payments, technology and the development of particular sectors or activities. However, as the achievement of such objectives via the use of performance requirements may require alterations to investment projects, investment incentives may be offered to offset resulting additional costs, the view being that the resource benefits to the country outweigh additional exchequer costs.

The other major motivation for performance requirements, to some extent related to the latter objective, is to counter perceived practices of multinational enterprises (e.g., transfer pricing, procurement practices, and other intra–enterprise arrangements) felt to be contrary to the interests of the host country. Thus, for example, product mandating requirements may be used to counter particular marketing strategies or local content requirements imposed to counter procurement practices. Not only is it difficult to distinguish between measures taken for this motivaiton as opposed to that concerning the achievement of certain national economic objectives, but it is also likely that, even when the "countering distortive practices" motivation is clear, investment incentives may well still be offered to "sugar the pill" of requirements and encourage the investment to be made.

This discussion may shed some light on the effects of the package of incentives and disincentives on international direct investment and the relative influences played by different measures[45]. At the aggregate level, the principal factors influencing the location of international direct investment are market prospects and cost factors, with the role played by investment incentives and disincentives being generally of a secondary nature. However, once a broader view is taken of incentives, particularly when trade protection measures are included, a much more significant influence can be ascribed to incentives, as these types of measures are closely associated with market attraction and prospects. As suggested above, the strength of this attraction may be such that it permits or facilitates the use of performance requirements, in which case the latter cannot be seen as a primary determinant of location. However, it has also been noted that performance requirements may have an independent locational impact, as for example, when they result in additional, defensive investments. The main role ascribed in the above argument for investment incentives is therefore that of offsetting the costs resulting from performance requirements.

Of course, particular types of performance requirements or the levels at which they are set may be regarded by business as unacceptable, or the level of awards in investment incentive schemes may be seen as insufficient compensation, in which case the investment may be abandoned, relocated or altered in some other manner. The above discussion of the impact of disincentives for specific sectors provides examples of particular cases where this has happened.

In other cases, it may be that performance requirements and incentives largely cancel each other out (just as similar investment incentive provisions between different countries may neutralise their effect on influencing the choice of location between the countries concerned) such that the investment goes ahead. However, it is often likely that the characteristics of that investment (e.g., in respect of size, organisational structure, purchasing and trading patterns) may be different from those which would have arisen from a situation of no incentives and no requirements.

Although incentives and disincentives may, in some sense or another, cancel each other out, the assessment by business of the impact of these measures is not simply one of finding equivalent values for different measures and calculating some net financial effect. As noted above, incentives and disincentives may be perceived very differently by business; it is one thing to assist investors to do what they would like to and an entirely different matter to restrict or prohibit it, or to impose requirements on how it should be carried out.

*

*   *

As seen from the above discussion, disincentives, in comparison with investment incentives, are likely to have a wider impact on international direct investment decisions; they are more closely associated with investors' perception of the business climate, their impacts on investment may be more diverse and they can influence more components of the overall international direct investment decision (e.g., the decision to undertake international direct investment over exports, the form and other characteristics of the investment and its timing) in addition to its location. While there are few studies examining the exact impact of disincentives on investment decisions, those which do lend support to the above analysis, although they are careful to point out situations where they may have very significant or minor impacts or on what basis (methodology, coverage, etc.) their conclusions are reached. Furthermore, these measures, and this is also true for investment incentives, may still have important effects on trade flows or on resource allocation even in the absence of effects on investment (while the existence of investment effects obviously results in trade effects through import substitution or export generation). Indeed the measures concerned would generally affect the costs or benefits attached to a particular project, even though they may not be sufficient to modify the investment aspects of the project (size, timing, location, etc.). Trade effects of the measures concerned are thus, in general, to be seen as more prevalent than investment effects.

Throughout the 1970s and until the 1980s a number of countries, particularly developing countries, increased their use of performance requirements, perhaps to some extent as they felt more or less guaranteed of a certain level of international direct investment and thus concentrated efforts in maximising host country benefits through the use of performance requirements. Since then, there are indications in a number of countries of relaxation in their disincentives regimes. For example, and as shown in a recent OECD study on the NICs[46], countries such as Korea and Taiwan have been taking steps to reduce the number of restrictions on international direct investment — Korea has relaxed its system of investment authorisation and Taiwan has reduced the scope of its previously wide (minimum of 50 per cent of output) system of export requirements. In other countries this trend is likely to be more closely associated with the pronounced deceleration of international direct investment in

62

developing countries and particularly in Latin America, with difficulties resulting from the debt situation, and ensuing problems of conducting business, a changing appreciation of the contribution that international direct investment may make to development and also therefore of the appropriate means to encourage it. It is also likely that a role is played by the fact that the negative effects of such measures are heightened in periods of slow growth and greater risk and uncertainty and would therefore result in stronger disincentive effects at a time when attention is turning more to attracting rather than controlling multinational enterprises. In a sense, this can be seen as a parallel with the trend discussed in Section 2 above concerning competition between countries for international direct investment by the use of investment incentives which may now have dampened down and where the approach may increasingly be one of attracting international direct investment by relaxing or removing disincentives.

Notwithstanding this, there are other examples where countries have maintained or even increased their use of measures that have a disincentive impact on investment flows[47]. In Brazil, for example, and despite a deteriorating situation, restrictions on foreign investment have generally been maintained if not increased in areas such as, for example, measures in the area of high technology, including reserved markets, although there has been some relaxation on local ownership requirements (from 100 per cent to 70 per cent) in high technology activities. In Mexico legislation proposing relaxation has been discarded and while increasing possibilities for majority foreign ownership are now offered, measures have also been introduced which have increased local content requirements or which have had the effect of reducing the security of patent protection. Furthermore, a number of heavily indebted countries, which may have been relaxing their foreign investment regulations, have been led to adopt other types of measures, aimed at forestalling capital or current outflows such as, for instance, import limitations on equipment or profit repatriation limitations, which may have significant effects on investment decisions. While some of these measures are intended to be, and hopefully will be of short duration, it is nevertheless clear that as long as they are in operation they will continue to seriously impede international direct investment.

Trends in the use of performance requirements over the next few years, especially in developing countries, cannot be easily predicted. While some countries may undertake or consolidate relaxations, others, particularly if their economic situation continues to deteriorate, may maintain or even expand requirements to obtain the maximum benefits from the investment they already have, although if pursued excessively, even captive investments may in the end decide to pull out. If world economic growth resumes at a substantial pace, the question will arise as to whether certain relaxations will be maintained or whether there will be a return to the policy approaches of the 1970s. Finally the outcome of the Uruguay Round negotiations may have a significant bearing on these issues.

NOTES AND REFERENCES

1. OECD "International Investment and Multinational Enterprises: Investment Incentives and Disincentives and the International Investment Process", Paris, 1983.

2. OECD "Controls and Impediments Affecting Inward Direct Investment in OECD Member Countries", Paris, 1987.

3. See, for example, "National Legislation and Regulations relating to Transnational Corporations", various volumes; United States Trade Representative (1985) "Barriers to Investment" and (1986) "Foreign Trade Barriers".

4. Agarwal, J.R. (1986) "Home Country Incentives and Foreign Direct Investment in ASEAN Countries", Kiel Working Paper No. 258.

5. For a recent discussion on regional policy and its effects, see OECD "Restructuring the Regions: Analysis, Policy Model and Prognosis", Paris, 1986.

6. Guisinger, S. and Associates (1985) "Investment Incentives and Performance Requirements", Praeger, New York.

7. World Bank (1984) "Investment Incentives for Industry: Some Guidelines for Developing Countries", Staff Working Papers.

8. Wells, L.T. (1986) "Investment Incentives: An Unnecessary Debate", CTC Reporter, No. 22, Autumn.

9. See, World Bank (1984) *op. cit.,* and Halback, A.J., Osterkamp, R. and Riedel, J. (1981) "Investment Policies of Developing Countries and their Repercussions on the Behaviour of German Enterprises", IFO Institute, Munich.

10. Root, F.R. and Ahmed, A.A. (1978) "The Influence of Policy Instruments on Manufacturing Direct Foreign Investment in Developing Countries", Journal of International Business Studies.

11. Hagaki, T. (1979) "Theory of the Multinational Firm: An Analysis of the Effects of Government Policies", International Economic Review, June.

12. Group of Thirty (1984) "Foreign Direct Investment", 1973–87.

13. Lim, D. (1983) "Fiscal Incentives and Direct Foreign Investment in Less Developing Countries", Journal of Development Studies, Volume 19, No. 2.

14. Nankani, G.T. (1979) "The Intercountry Distribution of Direct Foreign Investment in Manufacturing", Garland, New York.

15. Buckley, P.J. and Pearce, R.D. (1981) "Market Servicing by Multinational Manufacturing Firms: Exporting versus Foreign Production", Managerial and Decision Economics, 2, pp. 229–246.

16. Lim, D. (1983) *op. cit.*

17. Carson, M. and Pearce, R.D. (1986), "Multinational Enterprises in LDCs, in Multinationals and World Trade: Vertical Integration and the Division of Labour in World Industries", Allen and Unwin.

18. Agarwal, J.P. (1986) *op. cit.*

19. Guisinger, S. (1985) *op. cit.*

20. For more details, see OECD "International Investment and Multinational Enterprises: Recent Trends in International Direct Investment", Paris 1987.

21. Hufbauer, G.G. and Clapp, A.E. (1979) "International Aspects of State Tax and Expenditure Policies".

22. Dunning, J.H. (1983) "Changes in the Level and Structure of International Production: the last 100 years" in Casson, M.C., The Growth of International Business, Allen and Unwin.

23. OECD "Economic Performance and Structural Adjustment", Paris 1987.

24. OECD "Taxation in Developed Countries", Paris, 1987.

25. Frisch, D.J. and Hartman, D.G. (1983) "Taxation and the Location of U.S. Investment Abroad", NBER Working Paper No. 1241.

26. Vernon, R. (1979) "Storm over the Multinationals", Harvard University Press, Cambridge.

27. Fullington (1984) "Taxation of Income from Capital", NBER.

28. See Wall, D. (1976) "Export Processing Zones" Journal of World Trade Law, 10 pp. 478–489 and Basile, A. and Germidis, D., "Investment in Free Export Processing Zones", OECD Development Centre.

29. Kreye, O., Heinricks, J. and Fröbel, F. (1987) "Export Processing Zones in Developing Countries: Results of a Survey", ILO Working Paper No. 43.

30. Maex, F. (1983) "Employment and Multinationals in Asian Export Processing Zones", ILO Working Paper No. 26.

31. See, Warr, P.G. (1983) "The Jakarta Export Processing Zone: Benefit and Cost", Bulletin of Indonesian Economic Studies, 19 pp. 28–49, and Warr, P.G. (1984) "Korea's Mason Free Export Zone: Benefit and Costs", The Developing Economies, 22 pp. 169–185.

32. Dror, D.M. (1984), "Aspects of Labour Law and Relations in Selected Export Processing Zones", International Labour Review, 123, pp. 705–723.

33. Balasubramanyam, V.N. and Rothschild, R. (1985) "Free Port Zones in the United Kingdom", Lloyds Bank Review, No. 158, October.

34. OECD "Controls and Impediments Affecting Inward Direct Investment", *op. cit.*

35. OECD "The Code of Liberalisation of Capital Movements", Paris 1986. See also, OECD "Introduction to the OECD Codes of Liberalisation", Paris 1987.

36. See Guisinger, S. (1986), "Do Performance Requirements and Investment Incentives Really Work?", The World Economy 9.1 March, and Vukmanic, F.G. (1982) "Performance Requirements: The General Debate and a Review of Latin American Practices".

37. See, Conference Board (1983) "Operating Foreign Subsidiaries", Report No. 836.

38. See Zakour, A. (1981) "The Use of Investment Incentives and Performance Requirements by Foreign Governments". International Trade Administration, U.S. Dept. of Commerce.

39. In this respect, it may be noted that the Trade Committee is currently looking at the trade effects of trade–related investment measures.

40. See, for example, Guisinger and Associates (1985) *op. cit.* and The Conference Board (1983), *op. cit.*

41. See, Dunning, J.H. (1981) "International Production and the Multinational Enterprise", Allen and Unwin, and Buckley P.J. and Casson M.C. (1985) "Economic Theory of the Multinational Enterprise, Selected papers", chapters 1 and 2, Macmillan.

42. The Conference Board (1983) *op. cit.*

43. See Guisinger, S. (1985) *op. cit.*

44. See Safarian, A.E. (1982) "Trade–Related Investment Issues", Trade Policy in the Eighties Conference Paper.

45. *Ibid.*

46. OECD "The Newly Industrialising Countries: Challenge and Opportunity for OECD Industries", Paris, 1988.

47. See Vukmanic, F.G. (1982) *op. cit.*

Annex

DISINCENTIVES, INCLUDING
TRADE–RELATED INVESTMENT MEASURES,
IN DEVELOPING COUNTRIES

The following table summarises the information available on the incidence of trade–related and other measures with disincentives effects in developing countries. It is based on a number of sources, and in particular the report on Barriers to Investment by the Office of the U.S. Trade Representative, 1985. The information presented in this table is of a very tentative nature and should not be regarded as complete or precise either with respect to its comprehensiveness, the exact nature of the measures or the manner in which they are implemented.

Country	Sector	Type of measure[1] [2]			
		LC	EX	TT	LE
1. Central and South America					
Argentina	All			X	
	Automotive	X			
	Informatics				X*
Barbados	All	X			
Bolivia	All	X		X	
Brazil	All	X,X*		X*	
	Informatics	X			
	Automotive	X*			
	Various	X			X
	Telecommunications				X
Chile	Automotive	X			
Columbia	All		X,X[1]	X,X[1]	
	Automotive	X			
	Electronics	X	X		
Costa Rica	All	X*			
Dominican Republic					
Ecuador	All	X*			X
	Agriculture		X*		
	Automotive	X			
	Construction				X
	Finance				X
	Manufacturing	X			
Haïti					

67

Country	Sector	Type of measure[1] [2]			
		LC	EX	TT	LE
Jamaica					
Mexico	All	X,X*	X	X	X,X[1]
	Automotive	X	X		X
	Pharmaceutical/ chemical/electronics	X	X		
Panama	Light assembly	X*			
Paraguay	All		X*		X
Peru	All				X,X[1]
	Automotive	X			
Trinidad/Tobago					
Uruguay	Automotive	X,X[1]	X		
Venezuela	All	X,X*			X,X*
	Accountancy				X
	Automotive	X	X,X[1]		
	Banking				X
	Cigarettes	X			
	Electronics	X			
	Insurance				X,X*
	Services				X

2. Middle East and Asia

Country	Sector	Type of measure[1] [2]			
Bangladesh	All		X*		
	Pharmaceuticals	X	X		
China	All	X	X		X
India	All	X,X[1]	X	X,X*	X
Indonesia	All	X			X,X[1]
	Various sectors	X			
Iraq					
Kuwait	All				X
Malaysia	All	X,X*	X,X*		X,X[1]
	Insurance				X
	Motor cycles	X			
Pakistan	All	X			
Philippines	All			X	X
	Automotive	X			
Saudi Arabia	All				
Singapore					
South Korea	All	X,X*	X,X*		X
	Automotive	X	X		
Sri Lanka	All	X*	X*		X
Taiwan	All	X,X*	X		
	Agri-machinery	X			
	Automotive	X			
	Bicycle/ motorcycle	X			

Country	Sector	Type of measure[1] [2]			
		LC	EX	TT	LE
Taïwan	Telephones	X			
	Television	X			
Thailand	All				X,X*
	Banking/finance				X
	Various				X
	Automotive	X			
3. Africa					
Burkina Faso	All	X,X*			
Burundi					
Central African Republic	All	X			
Egypt	All	X,X*	X*		
	Automotive	X			
Ethiopia	Various				X
Gambia					
Ghana	All	X	X		
	Banking				X
	Insurance				X
	Manufacturing	X			
	Natural resource exploitation				X
Guinea	Natural resource exploitation				X
Ivory Coast	Certain sectors				X
	Manufacturing	X			
Liberia					
Mali	All	X*			
Morocco	All	X			
	Automotive	X			
	Services				X
Mozambique	All				X
Niger	All	X			X*
Nigeria	All	X*			X
Rwanda					
Senegal					
Sierra Leone					
Somalia					
Sudan	All	X			
Tanzania	All	X			X
Togo	All				X*
Tunisia	All		X,X*		X¹
Zaire	All	X			
Zambia	All	X*			
Zimbabwe	All	X	X		

1. LC – local content, local sourcing, import requirements.
   EX – export requirements.
   TT – transfer of technology requirements.
   LE – local equity ownership requirements.
2. Measures marked X* denotes measures linked to the award of incentives; measures marked X¹ denotes measures linked to the removal/relaxation of other requirements.

WHERE TO OBTAIN OECD PUBLICATIONS
OÙ OBTENIR LES PUBLICATIONS DE L'OCDE

ARGENTINA - ARGENTINE
Carlos Hirsch S.R.L.,
Florida 165, 4º Piso,
(Galeria Guemes) 1333 Buenos Aires
Tel. 33.1787.2391 y 30.7122

AUSTRALIA - AUSTRALIE
D.A. Book (Aust.) Pty. Ltd.
11-13 Station Street (P.O. Box 163)
Mitcham, Vic. 3132   Tel. (03) 873 4411

AUSTRIA - AUTRICHE
OECD Publications and Information Centre,
4 Simrockstrasse,
5300 Bonn (Germany)   Tel. (0228) 21.60.45
Gerold & Co., Graben 31, Wien 1 Tel. 52.22.35

BELGIUM - BELGIQUE
Jean de Lannoy,
Avenue du Roi 202
B-1060 Bruxelles   Tel. (02) 538.51.69

CANADA
Renouf Publishing Company Ltd
1294 Algoma Road, Ottawa, Ont. K1B 3W8
Tel: (613) 741-4333
Stores:
61 rue Sparks St., Ottawa, Ont. K1P 5R1
Tel: (613) 238-8985
211 rue Yonge St., Toronto, Ont. M5B 1M4
Tel: (416) 363-3171
Federal Publications Inc.,
301-303 King St. W.,
Toronto, Ont. M5V 1J5   Tel. (416)581-1552
Les Éditions la Liberté inc.,
3020 Chemin Sainte-Foy,
Sainte-Foy, P.Q. G1X 3V6,   Tel. (418)658-3763

DENMARK - DANEMARK
Munksgaard Export and Subscription Service
35, Nørre Søgade, DK-1370 København K
Tel. +45.1.12.85.70

FINLAND - FINLANDE
Akateeminen Kirjakauppa,
Keskuskatu 1, 00100 Helsinki 10   Tel. 0.12141

FRANCE
OCDE/OECD
Mail Orders/Commandes par correspondance :
2, rue André-Pascal,
75775 Paris Cedex 16   Tel. (1) 45.24.82.00
Bookshop/Librairie : 33, rue Octave-Feuillet
75016 Paris
Tel. (1) 45.24.81.67 or/ou (1) 45.24.81.81
Librairie de l'Université,
12a, rue Nazareth,
13602 Aix-en-Provence   Tel. 42.26.18.08

GERMANY - ALLEMAGNE
OECD Publications and Information Centre,
4 Simrockstrasse,
5300 Bonn   Tel. (0228) 21.60.45

GREECE - GRÈCE
Librairie Kauffmann,
28, rue du Stade, 105 64 Athens   Tel. 322.21.60

HONG KONG
Government Information Services,
Publications (Sales) Office,
Information Services Department
No. 1, Battery Path, Central

ICELAND - ISLANDE
Snæbjörn Jónsson & Co., h.f.,
Hafnarstræti 4 & 9,
P.O.B. 1131 - Reykjavik
Tel. 13133/14281/11936

INDIA - INDE
Oxford Book and Stationery Co.,
Scindia House, New Delhi 110001
Tel. 331.5896/5308
17 Park St., Calcutta 700016   Tel. 240832

INDONESIA - INDONÉSIE
Pdii-Lipi, P.O. Box 3065/JKT.Jakarta
Tel. 583467

IRELAND - IRLANDE
TDC Publishers - Library Suppliers,
12 North Frederick Street, Dublin 1
Tel. 744835-749677

ITALY - ITALIE
Libreria Commissionaria Sansoni,
Via Benedetto Fortini 120/10,
Casella Post. 552
50125 Firenze   Tel. 055/645415
Via Bartolini 29, 20155 Milano   Tel. 365083
La diffusione delle pubblicazioni OCSE viene
assicurata dalle principali librerie ed anche da :
Editrice e Libreria Herder,
Piazza Montecitorio 120, 00186 Roma
Tel. 6794628
Libreria Hœpli,
Via Hœpli 5, 20121 Milano   Tel. 865446
Libreria Scientifica
Dott. Lucio de Biasio "Aeiou"
Via Meravigli 16, 20123 Milano   Tel. 807679

JAPAN - JAPON
OECD Publications and Information Centre,
Landic Akasaka Bldg., 2-3-4 Akasaka,
Minato-ku, Tokyo 107   Tel. 586.2016

KOREA - CORÉE
Kyobo Book Centre Co. Ltd.
P.O.Box: Kwang Hwa Moon 1658,
Seoul   Tel. (REP) 730.78.91

LEBANON - LIBAN
Documenta Scientifica/Redico,
Edison Building, Bliss St.,
P.O.B. 5641, Beirut   Tel. 354429-344425

**MALAYSIA/SINGAPORE -
MALAISIE/SINGAPOUR**
University of Malaya Co-operative Bookshop
Ltd.,
7 Lrg 51A/227A, Petaling Jaya
Malaysia   Tel. 7565000/7565425
Information Publications Pte Ltd
Pei-Fu Industrial Building,
24 New Industrial Road No. 02-06
Singapore 1953   Tel. 2831786, 2831798

NETHERLANDS - PAYS-BAS
SDU Uitgeverij
Christoffel Plantijnstraat 2
Postbus 20014
2500 EA's-Gravenhage   Tel. 070-789911
Voor bestellingen: Tel. 070-789880

NEW ZEALAND - NOUVELLE-ZÉLANDE
Government Printing Office Bookshops:
Auckland: Retail Bookshop, 25 Rutland Stseet,
Mail Orders, 85 Beach Road
Private Bag C.P.O.
Hamilton: Retail: Ward Street,
Mail Orders, P.O. Box 857
Wellington: Retail, Mulgrave Street, (Head
Office)
Cubacade World Trade Centre,
Mail Orders, Private Bag
Christchurch: Retail, 159 Hereford Street,
Mail Orders, Private Bag
Dunedin: Retail, Princes Street,
Mail Orders, P.O. Box 1104

NORWAY - NORVÈGE
Narvesen Info Center - NIC,
Bertrand Narvesens vei 2,
P.O.B. 6125 Etterstad, 0602 Oslo 6
Tel. (02) 67.83.10, (02) 68.40.20

PAKISTAN
Mirza Book Agency
65 Shahrah Quaid-E-Azam, Lahore 3 Tel. 66839

PHILIPPINES
I.J. Sagun Enterprises, Inc.
P.O. Box 4322 CPO Manila
Tel. 695-1946, 922-9495

PORTUGAL
Livraria Portugal, Rua do Carmo 70-74,
1117 Lisboa Codex   Tel. 360582/3

**SINGAPORE/MALAYSIA -
SINGAPOUR/MALAISIE**
See "Malaysia/Singapor". Voir
«Malaisie/Singapour»

SPAIN - ESPAGNE
Mundi-Prensa Libros, S.A.,
Castelló 37, Apartado 1223, Madrid-28001
Tel. 431.33.99
Libreria Bosch, Ronda Universidad 11,
Barcelona 7   Tel. 317.53.08/317.53.58

SWEDEN - SUÈDE
AB CE Fritzes Kungl. Hovbokhandel,
Box 16356, S 103 27 STH,
Regeringsgatan 12,
DS Stockholm   Tel. (08) 23.89.00
Subscription Agency/Abonnements:
Wennergren-Williams AB,
Box 30004, S104 25 Stockholm Tel. (08)54.12.00

SWITZERLAND - SUISSE
OECD Publications and Information Centre,
4 Simrockstrasse,
5300 Bonn (Germany)   Tel. (0228) 21.60.45
Librairie Payot,
6 rue Grenus, 1211 Genève 11
Tel. (022) 31.89.50
Maditec S.A.
Ch. des Palettes 4
1020 - Renens/Lausanne   Tel. (021) 635.08.65
United Nations Bookshop/Librairie des Nations-
Unies
Palais des Nations, 1211 - Geneva 10
Tel. 022-34-60-11 (ext. 48 72)

TAIWAN - FORMOSE
Good Faith Worldwide Int'l Co., Ltd.
9th floor, No. 118, Sec.2, Chung Hsiao E. Road
Taipei   Tel. 391.7396/391.7397

THAILAND - THAILANDE
Suksit Siam Co., Ltd., 1715 Rama IV Rd.,
Samyam Bangkok 5   Tel. 2511630
INDEX Book Promotion & Service Ltd.
59/6 Soi Lang Suan, Ploenchit Road
Patjumamwan, Bangkok 10500
Tel. 250-1919, 252-1066

TURKEY - TURQUIE
Kültur Yayinlari Is-Türk Ltd. Sti.
Atatürk Bulvari No: 191/Kat. 21
Kavaklidere/Ankara   Tel. 25.07.60
Dolmabahce Cad. No: 29
Besiktas/Istanbul   Tel. 160.71.88

UNITED KINGDOM - ROYAUME-UNI
H.M. Stationery Office,
Postal orders only: (01)873-8483
P.O.B. 276, London SW8 5DT
Telephone orders: (01) 873-9090, or
Personal callers:
49 High Holborn, London WC1V 6HB
Branches at: Belfast, Birmingham,
Bristol, Edinburgh, Manchester

UNITED STATES - ÉTATS-UNIS
OECD Publications and Information Centre,
2001 L Street, N.W., Suite 700,
Washington, D.C. 20036 - 4095
Tel. (202) 785.6323

VENEZUELA
Libreria del Este,
Avda F. Miranda 52, Aptdo. 60337,
Edificio Galipan, Caracas 106
Tel. 951.17.05/951.23.07/951.12.97

YUGOSLAVIA - YOUGOSLAVIE
Jugoslovenska Knjiga, Knez Mihajlova 2,
P.O.B. 36, Beograd   Tel. 621.992

Orders and inquiries from countries where
Distributors have not yet been appointed should be
sent to:
OECD, Publications Service, 2, rue André-Pascal,
75775 PARIS CEDEX 16.

Les commandes provenant de pays où l'OCDE n'a
pas encore désigné de distributeur doivent être
adressées à :
OCDE, Service des Publications. 2, rue André-
Pascal, 75775 PARIS CEDEX 16.

72380-1-1989

OECD PUBLICATIONS, 2, rue André-Pascal, 75775 PARIS CEDEX 16 - No. 44749 1989
PRINTED IN FRANCE
(21 89 02 1) ISBN 92-64-13216-3